Understand Your
DREAMS NOW

Spiritual Dream Interpretation

Understand Your
DREAMS NOW
Spiritual Dream Interpretation

Doug Addison

Understand Your Dreams Now: Spiritual Dream Interpretation
By Doug Addison

ISBN 13 - 978-0-9824618-4-6
ISBN 10 - 0-9824618-4-4

Printed in USA by:
InLight Connection
PO Box 7049
Santa Maria, CA 93456

Cover design by Cathy Arkle.
Interior layout design by eGenCo.

For ordering information contact:
InLight Connection
(800) 507-7853
www.DougAddison.com

ENDORSEMENTS

With many years of experience, the wisdom of an ancient sage is mixed with relevancy of a contemporary prophetic spokesman in the writings of Doug Addison. This man's understanding ranks among the top in this generation for "interpretive skills." Deep, yet user friendly!

James W Goll
Encounters Network - Prayer Storm
Best Selling Author

Many today are dreaming significant dreams and yet lack understanding as to the interpretation. Doug Addison's skillfully written book is a valuable resource for those who are looking for answers, insight, and teaching into the subject of dreams and their interpretation. Doug teaches that you CAN interpret your dreams and the dreams of others.

Patricia King
Founder of XPministries
www.xpministries.com

Doug Addison's book, *Understand Your Dreams Now! Spiritual Dream Interpretation,* is a comprehensive guide that anyone can use to interpret what God is speaking to them in their own dreams, and also become a powerful minister assisting others to understand the language of dreams. I encourage you to begin your "dream journey" by allowing this book to be a training manual, and to use Doug's amazing journey and insights to help you along the way.

Randy Clark
Founder of Global Awakening
and The Apostolic Network of Global Awakening

DEDICATION
and Special Thanks:

I owe so much to my mentor and spiritual father, John Paul Jackson, who first trained me in dream interpretation. Also, my wife Linda, who encouraged me to pursue my dreams!

I would like to acknowledge and give special thanks to those who helped me develop, write, and edit this book: Nina Edwards, Robert Watson-Hemphill, Julianna LeRay, Michele Partain, Marti Statler, Arlene Brown, and countless others who helped in so many ways over the years.

CONTENTS

FOREWORD

The world is intrigued with the concept of communication with other life forms and the idea of interacting with multidimensional realities that might have the capacity to unveil the mysteries of our future. Scientists labor to unlock the secrets of parallel universes through quantum physics in hopes that these discoveries might reveal the destiny of the universe, and ultimately, its inhabitants. Millions of people are flocking to psychics, palm readers, and soothsayers to access their fate through the world of paranormal phenomena. Yet in the midst of all this, most people are completely unaware that God designed a way of reaching through the veil of eternity to communicate to His beloved people their future and destiny through the avenue of dreams.

Much like learning a foreign language or reading hieroglyphics, understanding dreams is a skill that can be acquired through teaching, instruction, and practice. So many gifted people find themselves troubled, confused, or even plagued by dreams because they misinterpret or misapply them, which often leads to the fear of someone's demise. Doug Addison has done a masterful job of clearly communicating, in a simple and understandable way, how to interpret your dreams and access your future now. This will bring peace to dreamers and open the door to new dimensions in your life. *Understand Your Dreams Now* is more than a book; it is a step-by-step training manual written to help you to comprehend these visions of the night.

In this powerful book, you will learn about several different types of dreams and their unique functions, how to understand symbols, and what to do about nightmares. Doug even has a chapter about teaching children the art of dream interpretation.

Doug Addison is uniquely qualified to write this book, having been trained and mentored by the famed dream interpreter, John Paul Jackson. Doug also has decades of experience helping people to accurately interpret their dreams. For years he has interpreted dreams for people in the streets, in churches, in bars and nightclubs, and in the marketplace. Doug has traveled the world doing seminars and conferences on dream interpretation. He's one of the most respected experts in this field. His insightful stories and straightforward writing style make this book applicable for the novice, yet his deep understanding and revelatory nature also make *Understand Your Dreams Now* a great resource for mature leaders with lots of experience.

Years ago I read a dream interpretation book, and I was so impacted by the author's life that I began to gather other dreamers weekly. We would journal our dreams during the week and then meet together to try our hand at interpreting them. At first, it was just a fun way of learning how to hear from God. But as the months passed, each of us was so deeply impacted by the mysteries that were being discovered through our dreams that nearly every single one of us was dramatically transformed. That experience leads me to believe that Doug Addison's book could actually cause a radical revolution both to the reader and to the world around them.

God said that, "In the last days ... [He] ... would pour out His Spirit on everyone ..." in the world. This heavy rain would result in people having visions and dreams. Think about the ramifications of billions of people suddenly hearing the clarion voice of their Creator and supernaturally comprehending His deep love for them! We are actually in the midst of that very epoch that was foretold long ago by the prophet Joel. Joel's prophecy makes this book a *must-read* for every Christian, and for that matter, every dreamer on the planet.

I highly recommend this book. I have the deepest respect for the author and his insights. May God meet you in the pages of this book and lead you into the palace of your dreams!

Kris Vallotton
Senior Associate Leader, Bethel Church, Redding, California
Co-Founder of Bethel School of Supernatural Ministry
Author of nine books including
The Supernatural Ways of Royalty and *Spirit Wars*

INTRODUCTION

Are you ready to journey into the amazing world of dreams and the supernatural? You picked up this book curious to learn what goes on behind that shadowy door of supernatural happenings in your mind at night. Let me take you on an exciting ride into the world of dreams and how to interpret them. It'll be fun, and surprisingly quick and easy!

This book could very well change your life forever. I can help you understand the hidden meaning in dreams—and do it quickly.

Would you believe that by interpreting dreams, you might save your own life, meet your future spouse, make the right business move at work, learn the callings of your children, see what can take place ahead of time, or help you be at the right place at the right time? It does happen.

What you will learn

This book is full of inside tips and secrets that I have learned after interpreting tens of thousands of dreams and training thousands of dream interpreters over the past twenty years. Here's a sample of what you will learn about dreams:

- to get the meaning quickly with pinpoint accuracy
- to recognize symbolic messages in dreams and from movies, television shows, music, art, and nature

- to develop your ability to hear God through your dreams and daily life
- which dreams are important to pay attention to
- how to respond to dreams to change your life for the good
- to find dreams that give you clues about your destiny and life calling
- turn around a negative dream or nightmare to get a positive outcome
- how to track and journal your dreams

Have you ever dreamed of flying, falling, running or being chased, having a baby, teeth coming loose, showing up without your clothes, or going to the bathroom in public … ? These are some of the many Common Dreams people have that actually have significant meanings. You will be able to take almost any dream, get its meaning, and apply it to your life.

We will also dive deep into the subject of scary dreams, and you'll find that not all nightmares are bad. You can learn to take a negative dream and actually positively change your waking life. Dreams are interactive, and once you understand them you will be equipped to help people around you as well.

This is a practical, how-to book, and I have included sample dreams and exercises. I will even give you a list of the meanings of some of the most popular dream symbols to help you get started. I have purposely kept the chapters short and will not overwhelm you with too much detail, as this process is better "caught than taught."

An amazing discovery

I have studied dream interpretation for decades and trained thousands of people on how to understand their dreams. One day, a colleague of mine asked how I was able to get to the meaning of a dream quickly and with what seemed like minimal effort. My ability to understand dreams this way came after years of study and practice, so the question I asked myself was: "How could I help people grasp dream interpretation faster than it had taken me?"

This sent me on a journey to eventually discover the most important things to look for in a dream that allow you to quickly understand its meaning. I had hundreds of hours of study and practical training in dream interpretation. I wanted to take the essence of my years of training and what I specifically look for as a dream expert. I also wanted to find a way to teach people this process that would allow them to catch on in less time.

After careful study of my own dream interpretive process, I determined that good dream interpreters do not rely only on dream symbol books. They have trained themselves to recognize the important symbolic elements in each dream. They realize that the meaning of symbols may change from dream to dream and dreamer to dreamer. They do not just use a method but also are intuitively perceptive to recognize the hidden messages. They can hear God speaking through dreams because ultimately, God is the giver of revelation. Plus, great dream interpreters have acquired on-the-job experience with interpreting dreams.

So I developed a theory on how to train people more quickly and ran it through several test groups. Every test group intuitively grasped dream interpretation much more quickly than those I had trained previously with more detail. In fact, many people who applied four to eight hours of my new way to understand dreams were often much further along than others who have studied for years, although all dream interpreters still need practice and experience to mature and get really good. These study groups were so successful that in 2007 I developed a live training workshop called *The Dream Crash Course* that went on the road for five years as I perfected the process. This book is a hybrid of all my years of experience interpreting dreams, training others, and doing countless outreaches.

I have gathered many of the ideas and concepts in this book from many sources over the years. I owe a lot to John Paul Jackson who paved the way for many of us dream interpreters who are now taking this message to the world. Much of what I learned and I am sharing in this book comes from my years as an instructor and dream team coordinator with Streams Ministries International.[1]

To make this a truly interactive book I've developed a corresponding website called www.UnderstandYourDreamsNow.com where you can download a dream journal and exercises, watch demonstration videos, and get additional dream resources.

Grace's dream

Grace dreamed she was at a concert dancing to an obscure song the musicians played from their repertoire. As she was enjoying the song, she came face to face with a young blond man she didn't recognize. She kissed him. The very next day, she attended that group's concert with friends and heard the very song from her dream. At that moment, she looked over and came face to face with a young blond man similar to her dream (no, she didn't kiss him) but years later, these two would marry and have three children. Grace said that the dream opened her eyes to noticing him.

Whether you are an experienced dream interpreter or just starting out, I know you will benefit from these concepts, practical training, and examples. This is what I wish someone would have shared with me when I was just starting out. I would have shaved years off my learning curve and saved myself a lot of frustration. If you apply what I share, you will be surprised at how quickly you will catch on to dream interpretation. Ultimately, we must rely on God to understand revelation but you can practice to perfect your abilities.

Are you ready to start the journey?

---

1   Streams Ministries International: www.streamsministries.com

CHAPTER 1

Breakthrough Dreams

"One of the most adventurous things left us is to go to bed. For no one can lay a hand on our dreams."

E. V. Lucas

Understanding dreams can radically change your life!

I was test-driving a car with my wife, and the salesman was in the back seat. He asked me what I do for a living, and he seemed surprised when I told him that I teach people how to understand their dreams. He told me, "I have been having a strange recurring dream that has been bothering me. I keep dreaming about being at my father's funeral standing next to his casket." In real life his father had passed away a few years before. I told him that although the dream may seem dark, it actually had a positive meaning and purpose for his life. The dream indicated that he was close to his father. It also seemed to suggest that there was something his father had not completed in life that this salesman was destined to fulfill. I told him that I believed he would fulfill it at an even greater level by following in his footsteps.

He grabbed my arm and said, "You will not believe this. This is my last day at the car dealership because I am leaving my career as a salesman to become a farmer, and my father was a farmer." I went on to tell him that God had given the dream to him, and it indicated his destiny in life. As we got back to the showroom, he wanted me to tell his sales manager because his co-workers felt that his decision was crazy. He got on his cell phone with his wife, and as he told her about what I had said, tears fell from his eyes.

I had the strangest dream last night

How many conversations in your life have started with "I had the strangest dream last night?" People are fascinated with the movies that play in their heads while sleeping. Some believe that dreams predict the future. Others say dreams depict real life or are a manifestation of what we want to be, while others might attribute a strange dream to what they ate. I am convinced that dreams can connect us with a power greater than ourselves. They are supernatural in nature and can have lasting impact on our lives. Dreams are more than just strange occurrences while we sleep. They are interactive, predictive, and can actually bring healing and even lasting change to our waking lives.

One-third of our life is spent asleep. That means that during an average lifetime, twenty-five years can be spent dreaming. Every night, we dream an average of one to two hours, and some studies show we usually have several dreams per night. These dreams are valuable whether you remember them or not.

Everybody dreams but not everyone can remember them. Just because you cannot remember dreaming does not mean that you did not dream.

The dream world is fascinating—full of speculation, hope, and sometimes, even fear. We can wake up from a good dream feeling refreshed and hopeful. On the other hand, we can wake up from a bad dream feeling tense and apprehensive. I will show you in this book how to use even a negative dream to positively change your life. Here's an example from my own life.

Breakthrough dream

I was impacted by a recurring nightmare that tormented me during my teenage years. I would be dreaming, and suddenly I would be aware of an evil presence. Gripped with fear, I would try to run but would be stuck or only able to move in slow motion. Sometimes I would wake up literally running through my house screaming at the top of my lungs, scaring my family and later my roommates as well.

Just before my nineteenth birthday, I was so stressed out by the nightmare I could not take it any longer. I decided that the next time I had this nightmare I was going to force myself to stay dreaming and face it. When the nightmare occurred again, I stopped in my tracks and said to myself in the dream, "I am going to stay asleep, I am going to stay asleep!" This time I really did stay asleep and decided to turn around and take a look at what it was that had been chasing me all these years. As I did, it was like a scene from the movie *Poltergeist*. Objects in the room began to rise up and I found my own body starting to rise and hover as well. Though I was terrified I went with it, and suddenly I could see that beyond the dark evil figure was a blinding white light. I woke up in a pool of sweat, but I had total peace. Wow! I had just had a supernatural encounter with my fears and overcame something that was trying to hold me back from my destiny. I never had that nightmare again, and my life took a dramatic turn for the good.

What followed was a spiritual awakening in my life. I was nineteen years old, and at that moment, I fell to my knees right beside my bed and invited Jesus into my life and soon after began pursuing my spiritual life. I am not sure how you came to read this book and I want you to know that my purpose for writing it is not to preach to you or tell you what to believe. I'm convinced that there is probably something in your life or maybe in someone you know that needs a breakthrough. You can very well receive this in a dream!

Everything changed in my life after that breakthrough dream. It later dawned on me that there was a reason an evil force was pursuing me in my dreams for over seven years. Something did not want me to go on in life and tried to stop me. This is evident because now I help literally millions of people get through their fears and understand their dreams. For this reason I also specialize in recurring dreams and nightmares. I often wonder what would have happened had I not faced the nightmare.

That breakthrough dream took place over thirty years ago and inspired me to learn more about dreams. I have been an avid dreamer all my life, remembering dreams all the way back to age four, but this breakthrough dream intrigued me to know more. Since then, I have studied dream interpretation from various approaches and have been a dream interpreter for a number of years. I have found the spiritual approach to dream interpretation has the greatest impact. I was amazed at the difference when I used the metaphoric language from the Bible as opposed to a list of symbols in books. I began interpreting dreams much more accurately when I did it from a spiritual standpoint that takes into consideration dreams and visions and symbolism from the Bible. The Bible is actually full of symbolism and has many dreams already interpreted. There is also a wealth of metaphoric meaning in stories that Jesus told called parables.

I am convinced that God is speaking to all of us all the time. Dreams are one major way to hear and connect with God. Although not all dreams are divinely inspired, once you understand symbolic language, you can take just about any dream, find its meaning, and apply it to your life in some way.

Many dreams are spiritual

Throughout this book I will mention God, the Bible, and other spiritual references. As I stated previously, it is not my intention to tell you what to believe. No matter what faith you have, I hope this book helps open the supernatural world of dreams to you. I want to take you on an exciting journey that can totally change your life.

To that end, I am sharing all I have learned about dreams. After years of practice and eventually becoming a professional dream interpreter,

I mastered the ability to recognize symbolism not only in dreams, but also in waking life. Having interpreted well over 25,000 dreams, I have thousands of stories just like the one about the car salesman.

Breakthrough in dream learning

Rapidly changing technology allows us to take advantage of new strategies available in the areas of learning and education. In my case, I have been self-taught in computer programming, web design, music, writing, and public speaking, becoming quite successful without a degree or extensive training. Even though I did not attend college, I am honored that some of my books have been used in colleges. I realize that not everyone is wired like me, so I want to help you benefit from my quick method of learning as applied to dreams.

My strategy for learning has been to read what you need to know, find someone who is already doing what you want to do, and study how they do it. I became a computer network engineer and developed a very successful company in the San Francisco Bay area without a formal certification. I later applied this strategy and learned how to interpret dreams.

The book *Blink: The Power of Thinking Without Thinking* by Malcolm Gladwell, inspired me to find ways to learn quickly. Gladwell teaches that we can learn more quickly if we pattern ourselves after people who have mastered something. He called it "Thin Slicing"—learning from the masters. After studying people who are good at various things, he also concluded that we are actually more accurate when we spend less time thinking and instead react to the snap answers that pop into our heads. This reminded me of how spiritual intuitiveness really works. Once we learn to recognize the voice of God, we can train ourselves to quickly trust those small divinely inspired hunches.

Another streamlined method that stands out is the work of psychologist John Gottman. For over thirty years, Gottman and his team videotaped and studied couples interacting together. They observed people from all walks of life—some with good marriages and some with not-so-good marriages. After listening to a couple talk for one hour, Gottman was able to determine with an accuracy rate of 95% whether they were in danger of divorcing in the future if they did not get help. It was interesting to note that if he listened to them for two hours, his rate of accuracy actually went down to 90%. Later, he discovered that he actually only needs to hear a couple interacting for about three minutes to make an accurate diagnosis of their marital condition.

Gottman admits that he would be overwhelmed if he looked at every detail, so he trained himself to look for only four major factors. As he did this, he developed pinpoint accuracy in determining whether a couple will divorce if they do not get help. What are the four points? Well, you can read it for yourself in *The Seven Principles for Making Marriage Work: A Practical Guide from the Country's Foremost Relationship Expert.*

Gottman trained others to do the same by revealing his secrets as an expert and found that people could learn his process quite quickly. This really inspired me. As an expert dream interpreter, I have a high success rate of helping people accurately understand their dreams. I found that you don't have to look at all the details of a dream because you will become overwhelmed. In this book, you can learn from an expert and become skilled at determining what to look for in a dream that will make interpretation much easier.

Learning dream interpretation quickly

I explained my process of accelerated dream learning and how I've been able to teach thousands of people all over the world to understand their dreams more quickly. It took me years to learn all the details of dream interpretation, and I did it by studying and practicing. What I want to do for you is cut this learning time down considerably by giving you the things that I look for as an expert dream interpreter. I am going to give you these valuable insights at the beginning of this book instead of at the end, as it is commonly done. By doing this, you will be able to keep this in mind as you learn. I'll also go over these points again and again so they will become automatic for you, and you will no longer have to think about them.

I do not want to overwhelm you with a lot of information or facts about dreams. Information without practical application will not be helpful for you to learn how to interpret dreams. We are in a world that is on information overload, but we have little practical application for the information we receive. I know as we start talking about dream interpretation that there are many factors that go into it and it can get quite confusing, so I will show you exactly what I am looking for when I interpret a dream.

And of course, if you really want to master your ability to understand dreams, you must practice and study dreams, even if you don't know if you are doing it right. Practice, practice, practice! After years of interpreting dreams, I still record my dreams daily and take notes of new things that I learn. I keep my dream interpretation gift in shape by using it regularly. You cannot live on past successes only. Just like daily exercise, the minute that you stop using a talent or gift, you get out of shape and may not be as sharp.

I mentioned earlier the story of psychologist John Gottman, who studied couples interacting for over thirty years. He admitted that while assessing a couple, if he looked for all the things he knew that go into a good marriage and also make a marriage fail, he would be confused. But if he only looked at four important points, he could pinpoint problems at a 95% accuracy rate. It is the same with dream interpretation! Once you know what to look for in a dream, the meaning will almost stand out. Of course, we use revelation from God as well. Later, I'll explain more how these go hand-in-hand. First, we need to lay down some tracks to roll on so that we all get on the same page.

Since I am trying to simplify the complex process of dream interpretation and introduce to you a fast way to learn, I recommend finding ways to laugh. Yes, my advice to you is to lighten up as you read this book. I use comedy at my live events and find that people learn much more quickly while having a good time. For some reason, my comedy style does not always come across in my writing. You can go to www.

youtube.com and type in my name and you'll find some of my comedy videos. This will also help you get to know me better. I tend to be a little outside the box of normality.

As you may know, dreams come in many different categories and details. Perhaps at one time you too had a disturbing dream about a loved one that has passed on. Just like the car salesman I mentioned earlier, you may have a lingering question of what it all means. Possibly you have had a recurring nightmare that has left you covered in sweat, or maybe it is just a repetitious dream that has you wondering. Whatever it may be, I believe my book will open the door to understanding your dreams and finding the real truth behind them! Shall we begin?

CHAPTER 2

How to Fast-track

"If you can dream it, you can do it." Walt Disney

The world of dreams really is a strange place. Imagine for a moment what it's like to be a dream interpreter. Everywhere I go people are telling me their dreams! Even though many of them are long and somewhat bizarre, each person sharing is always into it. They go into a lot of detail to make sure you understand that the elephant they were riding backwards down the hallway was actually turquoise and not blue, and they were wearing a hat that looked like their grandfather's, but not really. Most of the time, they are not able to capture it in words since dreams reside in the spiritual realm. Dreams leave strong impressions even though people may not understand them.

When I first started out as a dream interpreter, I was really nervous and tried to keep track with the dreamer on every detail. I became confused and overwhelmed with all the aspects of their dreams. Later on, I learned to focus on just the important elements of the dream first. This made the process much easier.

I also realized that I had to learn to listen to people more closely. I don't know about you, but I am an easily distractible person. When it comes to listening to a dream, you can't drift off and find yourself thinking of something else in the middle of it. I benefited from taking a class and reading a book on some basic listening skills. You might want to consider practicing the art of listening if you want to become a good dream interpreter.

I told you I was going to give you the most important points to look for when interpreting a dream. Most books save the best for last, but I am going to bring it out right up front. There are four things that I look for when I interpret a dream. I wish someone had told me this a long time ago. I am showing you at the beginning of this process how I am able to interpret a dream very quickly. By doing this, you will begin to recognize the parts of dreams that matter the most and filter out things that are less detailed. I'm not trying to create a method but give you some insider advice from an expert that will make it much easier for you during your learning process. As a seasoned dream interpreter, I still follow this basic pattern, and I've trained thousands of dream interpreters to do the same. It will take away confusion and help you to know what to focus on. Here it is … drum roll please …

Four easy steps to dream interpretation[2]

 Who or what is the dream about, and what area of your life does it refer to?

 Is the dream positive or negative, and noticing the color, is it bright or dark?

 Are there any repeated themes, or is it a Common Dream?

 What are the three to four main points of the dream?

These are more questions to ask yourself as opposed to steps. Let's look at these four questions in detail so we can learn to interpret dreams.

---

2   Original concept derived from 201: Understanding Dreams and Visions course: www.streamsministries.com

QUESTION ONE:

Who or what is the dream about?

The very first thing you want to look for when it comes to dreams is who or what the dream is about. Are you the main character, or are you just involved, participating, or observing?

If you were the main character of the dream, the dream is most likely about you. If you are involved or participating, the dream is about you *and* something or someone else. If you are observing a situation in a dream, then most likely the dream is not about you, but about something else completely. Unless of course you are observing yourself, then the dream is still about you.

Observing dreams are usually about someone or something else. People who are particularly compassionate and like to care for others often have observing dreams. This is because they are getting insight on how to pray for people and support them. People with the gift of intercession often have dreams of observing so that they are motivated to pray.

What area of your life is the dream about?

Take note of the area of your life the dream is about. Often there will be people or places in the dream from your family, work, church, etc. Frequently, this will be a clue for context. If you are by yourself or in a place that you do not recognize, then the dream is most likely about you or some aspect of your life.

In addition to the role you play in the dream, it's important to look for the context of your life. Are you by yourself or with your family? Then it's probably mostly about you and having something to do with your family. Are you with people from work or school? Then it probably is related to your career or that area of your life. Are you with people from church or an organization that you belong to? Then the dream most likely relates to that area of your life.

Of course, this is a generalization and does not always apply to every single dream, but it is a good place to start. With all my experience, I have found that most dreams have people or places in them to tell you what area of your life that they point to. I call this a context anchor or clue, and it is helpful to pay attention to these details.

QUESTION TWO:

Is the dream positive or negative; is the color bright or dark?

The next thing to watch for is if the dream is positive or negative, and whether the colors are bright or dark. This will tell you about the source of the dream. The color of the dream can tell you how to make a practical application to your life. Positive dreams or dreams from God are usually bright or have some colors in them.

The thing that really matters is how you respond. Negative dreams are not all bad as they can reveal things in our lives that need to be changed. Later, you'll learn that when we see a negative dream, we need to flip it around and find the positive side that God is trying to point out. So in a sense, a negative dream can have a positive outcome.

Darker or muted color dreams tend not to be reality but show you things that need to be changed in your life. Black-and-white dreams are usually full of fear and similar to nightmares. What you should watch for are the dull or muted color dreams, as they are often plans of darkness against your life or maybe your own fears and not reality at all. They are dreams that show you how to pray and how to prepare and plan. Muted color or dark dreams may not be reality but more of a warning. In many cases, you will need to flip the meaning from negative to recognize a positive outcome.

Do not assume that all color dreams are from God and all black-and-white dreams are negative or from Satan. There's a lot more to it than that. But we do need to pay attention to whether the dream is positive or negative. That will help us later when we interpret and make a practical application to our daily lives.

People often ask me what a dream symbol means. For instance, they'll ask: "What does the color blue mean?" You may want to ask yourself: "Is it blue in the sky of a beautiful sunny day, or is it blue in the eye of a dinosaur that's about to eat me?" There is a big difference and this is called *context*. We will learn more about understanding context and how it can change from dream to dream.

QUESTION THREE:

Are there repeated themes, or is it a Common Dream?

Another major thing to watch for is repeated themes. This is the same thing said two times or more. It's the same thing said twice, it's the same thing said twice. Did you catch that? I'm repeating myself for dramatic effect. Sometimes themes repeat in a dream in order to highlight something important to pay attention to.

An example would be having a deflated beach ball and then walking to your car and seeing a flat tire. The repeated theme is loss of air. In dreams, air can represent aspects of your spiritual life. This dream may indicate that you need to increase your spiritual connection.

Repeated themes can also occur in different dreams over a period of time. It becomes easier to recognize this once you get into the habit of recording your dreams in a dream journal or on a computer on a regular basis. I will go into more detail on how to record your dreams and tips on journaling later.

Is this a Common Dream? Watch for dreams like these: flying, falling, running, having a baby, teeth coming loose, etc. The meaning may vary from dream to dream, but it will help you to recognize familiar themes. Many of these Common Dreams actually have a common meaning. We will get into the study of Common Dreams in Chapter 5 and become familiar with the dreams that lots of people have on a regular basis.

QUESTION FOUR:

What are three to four main points?

If you had to break the dream down to only three to four points what would they be? These are the main elements of the dream. Though a dream may be quite detailed, find just three or four main points that stand out in the dream. Even though there are often more than three to four points to the dream, it will help you quickly get the main meaning of the dream. It's like getting the interpretation into the crosshairs of a gun.

Did you know that your brain processes things in summary? If I asked you what you did last weekend, you would probably give me three to four main points and not go into all the details. We tend to summarize when we talk about things that we have done in the past. When Jesus taught parables, He gave simple explanations. Dreams are similar to night parables—we would lose too much of the meaning by looking too closely at details.

The problem with most new dream interpreters is they get too detailed and try to milk the dream for all it's worth. With dream interpretation "less is more," especially when you are learning. If you look at all the details in the dream you'll quickly get confused. To be a really good dream interpreter you will need to learn to do this as you look at a dream. Then, after you determine the actual interpretation or meaning of the dream, you can get into all the details and what is called the application or the purpose of the dream.

Let's try this process out on a dream.

Flying a kite dream

I dreamed that I was with a group of people from school and we were flying kites. A huge wind came and took my kite higher than all the others. I was trying to control the kite when it got tangled in some trees nearby. I was able to fly to the top of the trees and get the kite untangled. Back on the ground again, we all decided to go to the library to study.

When we got there a grand party was going on. I saw a girl I knew from elementary school. She came up and handed me a book and told me I would need this. I woke up.

Let's ask the four questions:

- Who or what is the dream about, and what area of your life does it refer to? The dream is about the dreamer and particularly his life involving school.

- Is the dream positive or negative, and noticing the color, is it bright or dark? It is a positive dream because even though the kite got stuck in the trees, he was able to get it untangled and the rest of the dream was good.

- Are there any repeated themes, or is it a Common Dream? Yes, there is a repeated theme of flying. He is flying a kite and the dreamer himself flies as well. One of the Common Dream themes is flying (without an airplane), and as you will find out later, it indicates a high calling or high creativity.

- What are the three to four main points of the dream? The main points of the dream are: flying the kite, the party at the library, and being given a book by the girl.

The interpretation of a dream

Once we know what the dream is about and where to focus, the actual dream interpretation should be quite short—three to five sentences, like a short paragraph—whenever possible. Too much detail in the interpretation may become confusing.

A good dream interpretation will state clearly the meaning of the dream without explaining the symbols. When we start to say flying is a high calling that you have, and the kite stuck in the trees is something you are trying to do that is getting stuck, and the library is symbolic of learning, and the book is knowledge you will need, then we might be adding too much detail to the interpretation. It is better just to say that the dream is about something you're being called to do that you are currently struggling with, but new revelation or knowledge is coming that will help you.

If you begin to tell people the meaning of the symbols during the interpretation, you will also give them the opportunity to disagree with you. Because many people already have a preconceived notion of the meaning of symbols, it is much better to have them hear the meaning of the dream and let it resonate with them first before discussing the details of the symbols. Stating the interpretation without explaining the symbols will also make you sound much more knowledgeable.

The final step is to develop a short, one paragraph, simple interpretation of the dream. You can use the three to four main points as a reference guide. Then, as you get better at it, you can develop your own style based on your gifts and uniqueness.

Some might think I am putting the cart before the horse by diving in so quickly into the "how to's" of dream interpretation. This is all part of the accelerated dream learning that I talked about in the last chapter. You know now where we are going and I am giving you the tools to think like a dream expert. As I said earlier in this chapter, there are four easy steps to interpreting dreams. If you follow the simple guidelines I have laid out for you and remember to listen closely to my helpful tips, in no time you too will be able to unravel the secrets whispered in the night. Next we will take a look at the biblical interpretive process that I have already introduced you to versus the popular methods of today.

CHAPTER 3

Freud, Jung, and Jesus

"Dreams are often most profound when they seem the most crazy."

Sigmund Freud

Freud, Jung, and Jesus

Dreams can be a very positive part of our lives. Understanding dreams correctly can be challenging since there are so many viewpoints out there that are often conflicting. Here's the test to know if your dream was interpreted correctly: you will feel a sense of connection or confirmation inside of you. Have you ever had someone try to give you the meaning of a dream you had, and it just does not sit right with you? Or it sounds too strange to coincide with the details you had given? Chances are it may not be the right meaning. Don't rule it out though, as the meaning of the dream might be challenging you to get beyond your current thinking or belief system.

Here are some key discoveries that have shaped dream interpretation, both positive and negative. Today, people tend to look at dreams from a psychological standpoint. Sigmund Freud and Carl Jung began teaching that dreams can reveal things about our core being that we are not aware of. They used dream interpretation as a means to psychoanalyze people. Freud taught that dreams tend to reveal our latent sexual desires, whereas Jung taught that most of the elements within a dream are there to reveal more about our inner-self. Both viewed dreams as a means of primarily revealing hidden clues to heal the psyche. They taught that the dream resides inside of you and is working its way out. Because of this belief, they often refer to dream interpretation as "dream work." Unfortunately, this is quite contrary to the spiritual Hebraic understanding that dreams come from the outside (God) and can reveal things within us, as well as things to come.

To their credit, Freud and Jung paved the way to make dreams more mainstream. Most people who have attended colleges or universities received Jungian dream interpretation training in a psychology class. Because of this, a therapy-based understanding of dreams tends to be the most popular viewpoint. Although there are elements of truth to what Freud and Jung taught, they do limit the world of dreams by seeing it primarily as a way to reveal the inner-self. Dreams can be healing but also very predictive and spiritually oriented. A dream can show you how to pray or prepare for a situation. It can be about your own struggles or even a life calling you have yet to fulfill.

You may ask, "What does Jesus have to do with it?" When I began to study dreams from a spiritual standpoint, I was drawn to the Bible, which is surprisingly packed full of dreams, visions, and symbolic language. Reading the stories of Joseph and Daniel, the two major dream interpreters in the Bible, has always impacted me, but what really got my attention was when I studied the teachings of Jesus. One of the things that Jesus said quite often is that we must have "eyes that see and ears that hear." He was referring to seeing and hearing spiritually. Jesus used parables, which are symbolic stories from real life situations that convey a deeper spiritual message about the Kingdom of God. Even His disciples who were close to Him did not understand this way of communication at first. You can learn a lot about God's hidden language by studying Jesus' parables.

What makes good dream interpreters so hard to find?

It's quite ironic that people everywhere are having dreams! People love talking about them and are eager to understand them, yet there is not much in the way of good dream interpretation training available today. What makes me say that? If there were good dream interpretation going on then we would not see literally billions of people walking around with no clue as to what their dreams mean. There are some major factors that have negatively affected the ability to accurately interpret our dreams.

I am convinced after all my study and on-the-street interaction with people that God can use dreams to help guide and speak to us. Not all dreams are from God, but many can have hidden meanings. A big part of hearing God through dreams requires trust and a step of faith. Many people have stopped believing that God can speak to us through dreams, so simply believing that it is possible can open dreams up in a greater way.

What negatively impacted dream interpretation?

A huge factor that has negatively impacted dream interpretation is that we tend to think logically. Dreams reside in the supernatural realm and do not always appear logical. Most people have a "western-world modern mindset" that the supernatural is not a normal part of life. Most of us did not grow up being taught how to understand the hidden meanings of our dreams. If we shared a bizarre dream we had, we were often laughed at or told to grow up.

Bookstores have a lot of dream symbol books. Many of us have been taught to use a list of dream symbols, but unfortunately, many of these books are not always accurate. Symbols vary from dream to dream, and some of the meanings may come from a psychological or even psychic dream understanding. In this book and at my live events, I do my best to train people how to understand and recognize symbolism and metaphors. I will present a short list of symbols at the end of this book to help you gain a baseline and for training purposes, but I do not recommend using symbol lists as a means of understanding dreams. You can use them as a starting place or to gain understanding, but be sure not to limit your interpretation too strictly on symbols.

Overall, dream interpretation has become a lost art. I have learned to use God's hidden language from the Bible as a basis for learning to understand symbolism. I realize that the Bible contains a broader message and is not to only be used as a means of symbolic understanding. Of course, not all symbols are always clearly defined in the Bible, so it helps to learn to recognize the patterns in how God speaks through symbolism. I was amazed when I began studying the Bible with new insight into this hidden language. I will walk you through some very fascinating discoveries and even how Jesus spoke in a hidden language as well. You will begin to recognize metaphors in your daily life that will help you better understand the dreams you have at night.

I had a dream no one can interpret

When people find out I am a dream interpreter, I most often hear, "I had a dream years ago that no one has been able to interpret." My response is usually, "You have to be kidding! I specialize in dreams that no one can interpret." There is a good chance that if no one has been able to interpret their dream, it is because the dream is from God or they have not met a good spirit-led dream interpreter.

Rising above dream

I was at a restaurant and struck up a conversation with a bunch of guys at the bar as I waited for my table. They found out I am a dream interpreter, and of course, one of them had a dream that no one had been able to interpret. The dream went like this: he was with his friends in a room and he kept sticking his thumb in his mouth and blowing. While doing this, he began to rise up to the top of the ceiling, hover there, and then come back down. He kept repeating this over and over. The meaning of the dream was that he has something greater to fulfill in his life and has potential, but his friends are holding him back. He keeps hitting a ceiling. I could see that my interpretation really moved him and that his friends sitting at the table were probably the ones who were holding him back. So, he walked outside with me and told me how that really impacted him and he agreed with me and gave me the opportunity to speak deeper into his life.

Dream interpreters in the Bible

Allow me to open up to you about the dreams, visions, and the supernatural in the Bible and how many people may have missed or at least misunderstood it. The purpose of this section is to take a fresh new look at how God speaks to us and gain some amazing insight into the symbolic, yet often hidden, language of God.

It is interesting that even though over one-third of the Bible is made up of dreams and visions, it is the last place most people think to go to learn about symbolism and metaphor. Although there are a lot of dreams and visions referenced, there are only a few actual dream interpreters mentioned. The two most influential ones are Joseph and Daniel in the Old Testament (also called the Jewish Torah).

Joseph

Most people know about Joseph as having a coat of many colors that was made for him by his father Jacob (Israel). Joseph was a dreamer from childhood and he had dreams about his future that took over twenty years to actually come to pass.[3] He dreamed that his brothers and his family would bow down at his feet. This caused his brothers to become jealous and fake Joseph's death and sell him to slave traders that took him to Egypt. Later, as God's destiny on his life unfolds, he finds himself standing in front of one of the most influential world leaders of his time. Pharaoh had two dreams that troubled him, and none of the astrologers

---

3   Genesis 37

or spiritual officials in Egypt could interpret them.[4] Just two years prior, Joseph had accurately interpreted the dreams of Pharaoh's cupbearer and baker.[5] This set him up to not only interpret Pharaoh's dreams, but also for him to be released from prison and placed as second in command in all of Egypt.

Joseph interpreted Pharaoh's dreams to mean that there would be seven years of plentiful times followed by seven years of intense famine. Joseph recommended a plan to store grain and provisions for the next seven years to prepare for the seven lean years. Things happened just as the dream foretold, and eventually, Joseph's family came and bowed at his feet just as he had dreamed as a child.

Daniel

Another amazing dream interpreter in the Bible was Daniel. It was during a time when Israel was captured and most Jewish people were living in exile under the Babylonians. King Nebuchadnezzar, the most powerful leader on earth at the time, had a dream. Similar to Pharaoh, none of the astrologers or wise men could interpret the king's dream. Nebuchadnezzar would not even tell people what the dream was and was requiring that someone had to prophetically tell him what he dreamed and the meaning of it. This was such a high order that no one was able to do it. Then Daniel heard about the situation and consulted some of his friends. In the middle of the night, God revealed the dream and its meaning to Daniel in a vision. As he shared it with the king, it was accurate and had so much impact on him that he placed Daniel in a high governmental position and lavished him with gifts.[6] Daniel later interpreted a nightmare plaguing the king and Daniel gave him advice that would have saved the king seven years of hardship had the king listened to him.[7]

---

4   Genesis 41
5   Genesis 40
6   Daniel 2
7   Daniel 4

It is interesting that the times when dream interpretation is mentioned, it was used to influence major world leaders and help change the course of history. In both cases, the popular dream interpretative method of that day could not interpret a dream from God. It is not like there was a lack of spiritual dream interpreters in ancient Egypt or Babylon, but there was a lack of people who could interpret a dream from God. This is still the case today with the psychological and psychic-based methods of interpreting dreams. These methods will not get a clear interpretation of a dream from God. It is also worth noting that both of these ungodly world leaders actually had a dream from God, and it took someone who could hear God's voice to interpret their dreams.

Hearing God and practicing

If you study the dream interpreters of the Bible more closely, you will find that both Joseph and Daniel indicated that they had to hear from God to get the interpretation.[8] What we do not see is that both of these guys had to practice and study as well as pray to God for the interpretations. In Daniel's case, he utilized a team.[9] I used to interpret dreams by just asking God what the dream meant. By doing this, our interpretations are limited to our ability to hear God clearly on any given day. You would never study the Bible by getting revelation from God alone. You can also use reference books and commentaries. This applies to dreams as well.

Later, I realized that even people in the Bible practiced and mentored with others. In the Jewish culture, it is very common to learn from a teacher. The prophet Samuel instituted the schools of the prophets in which he trained people to hear clearly. Jesus trained His disciples to understand parables. There is value in both hearing God directly to understand a dream and also practicing dream interpretation. It is also very helpful to practice and operate in a team like Daniel did.

---

8   Genesis 40:8, Daniel 2:27–28
9   Daniel 1:17 and 2:17-19

A new breed of dream interpreters

I believe that we are about to see an entirely new breed of people who can hear from God and interpret dreams. Just like Joseph and Daniel, we need trained people who can hear God's voice and are able to interpret the dreams of people—and possibly offer their help to government and world leaders. We also need dream interpreters to reveal strategies from God for businesses and to generate finances to fund new creative kingdom projects. Dreams will play a major role in the next decades to come. This is one of the major reasons why I have dedicated my life to training good dream interpreters. When people find out that you can interpret dreams accurately and hear the voice of God, they will invite you into businesses, media, and governmental meetings.

Why doesn't God just speak clearly?

I am talking a lot about hearing God through dreams, which may sound quite mysterious to some. People often say: "If God wants to speak to me, He will speak to me plainly." Those who are saying this obviously are not familiar with all the different and creative ways that God speaks through the Bible. Jesus didn't even speak plainly to His own disciples. The Bible is full of metaphor, symbolism, and hidden language. Even just reading the Bible requires some degree of interpretation.

God often conceals things so that those who are hungry and want to know more will search it out.[10] God will also hide things from people who consider themselves wise in their own eyes and reveal deep spiritual truths to those who are humble and childlike.[11]

Remember, to their credit, Freud and Jung paved the way to make dreams more mainstream, but God is the ultimate dream giver. God wants us to search and meditate on our dreams. He wants to remind us that just like Joseph and his coat of many colors, dreams are unique and hold the mysteries of the future. We must be sensitive to our own dreams

---

10   Proverbs 25:2
11   Matthew 11:25–26

and not take them for granted. We must have eyes that see and ears that hear, so that we can not only unravel what God is showing us for our own lives, but so that we can also encourage others!

In the next chapter, we will take a closer look at how God can speak to us through dreams. In particular, we'll look at the dreams and symbolism found in the Bible. I think you are going to be pleasantly surprised!

CHAPTER 4

Spiritual Dream Interpretation

"We both had dreams," they answered, "but there is no one to interpret them." Then Joseph said to them, "Do not interpretations belong to God? Tell me your dreams."

Genesis 40:8

I have been studying dream interpretation from a spiritual and biblical standpoint for decades. In doing so, I noticed that when we use the symbolism found in the Bible as a guideline and listen to God speak about the dream, we get a much deeper understanding. As I have trained thousands of dream interpreters, many of them are quite surprised at the positive results of this type of dream interpretation. Most of my experience has taken place in public places like festivals, malls, and large events in which we can have contact with a variety of different people. This gives me a broader understanding of dream symbols, as I have tested these symbols with people from all walks of life.

I have done a thorough study of dreams, visions, and the symbolism found in the Bible. Many of the dreams listed in the Bible already have interpretations provided for you. This is very useful in understanding how God speaks. Not all dreams are from God, but once we understand God's hidden symbolic language, an entirely new world opens up for us. We will not only see messages in the dreams that we have at night; we will also be able to hear God speaking to us in unlimited ways: on television, in the movies, street signs, names, and even numbers. The key to understanding dreams is using a combination of symbolic understanding and the ability to hear God's voice.

If you would like to do a study in the Bible, remember that the words *dream* and *vision* are often the same. You can use the Internet to search the Bible for dreams and visions. It is also helpful to study the book of Daniel and make a habit of reading the parables of Jesus. I don't believe that the Bible was meant to be used as a codebook to understand symbols. The best way to learn to hear God's voice is through a relationship with Him. But you can use the Bible to study symbolism, and in the process of doing so, you will understand much more about the nature and characteristic of God's love for people. Let's take a look at a few dreams, visions, and symbolic parables from the Bible.

King Nebuchadnezzar's dream

> *"These are the visions I saw while lying in my bed: I looked, and there before me stood a tree in the middle of the land. Its height was enormous. The tree grew large and strong and its top touched the sky; it was visible to the ends of the earth. Its leaves were beautiful, its fruit abundant, and on it was food for all. Under it the wild animals found shelter, and the birds lived in its branches; from it every creature was fed."*
> (Daniel 4:10–12)

Notice that the main character or point of focus of the dream is the tree, and the context is very positive. Its location, size, and impact had worldwide visibility. It supplied everyone with food and shelter. In the dream, there was no mention of the king. However, all of the aspects of the tree pointed toward someone with great power. This is a very good example of how Daniel recognized from the context of the dream that the tree was the king himself.

Other trees

"He (Jesus) took the blind man by the hand and led him outside the village. When He had spit on the man's eyes and put His hands on him, Jesus asked, 'Do you see anything?' He looked up and said, 'I see people; they look like trees walking around.'" (Mark 8:23–24)

From this we can determine that trees can sometimes represent people or leaders based on context, but not always. Notice other trees mentioned in the Bible: Tree of Life, Tree of the Knowledge of Good and Evil, and a tree planted by the water to name a few. We must look at the context of each of these to find out their meaning.

A good example of this is in the Garden of Eden where there were two trees.[12] One was the Tree of Life, and if you ate from it you would live forever. The other was the Tree of the Knowledge of Good and Evil. God told Adam not to eat from that tree. One was good, and one was not good for them, but the tree that was not good for them had the word *good* in it as well as evil. This is actually a symbolic message from God about two spiritual sources or voices that we can hear from. One of them is directly from God, and the other one has a mixture of good and evil. So as we learn to hear the voice of God, we must recognize the voice of the Holy Spirit and discern any other voices, which are often a mixture of our own good intentions and (sometimes) bad things.

Snakes

Snakes, for instance, usually represent lies and accusations. Notice that in Genesis Chapter 3, there is a snake in the Garden of Eden, and he lied and deceived Adam and Eve. Look at the function and context of snakes themselves. They slither around on the ground, and they have a

---

12   Genesis 2

forked tongue which could be symbolic of "talking out of both sides of their mouth" or split speech, also known as lying.

But like the two trees in the garden, there are also different types of snakes mentioned. Venomous snakes attacked the people of Israel, and God told Moses to make a bronze snake and put it up on a pole. If the afflicted people would look up at it they would live (Numbers 21:8–9). And as the people looked up to this bronze snake, God healed them. This was symbolic of the future coming of Christ who would be lifted up, and people would look to Him and be healed.

This is very interesting because it was originally a snake that lied and caused people to be separated from God. So later, when snakes attacked God's people, God used an image of a snake that had greater power and was symbolic of the future coming of Christ who would heal people that looked to Him.

So the question to ponder is when is a snake in a dream something negative, like lying, or positive, representing Christ and healing? The answer can be found in the context. Notice the snake in Genesis is deceiving people, and the bronze snake in Numbers is producing healing. In order for a snake in a dream to be positive, it would have to have some aspect of people getting healed. Instead, most snakes represent deception where people are lying against us. Even if we use a symbols list as a baseline, we still need to look at the function in the context of the symbol in the dream.

Dreams in the New Testament

There are many dreams and some good dream interpreters mentioned in the Old Testament of the Bible. There are also many dreams mentioned in the New Testament. It is interesting to note that you don't actually see someone who specializes in dream interpretation in the New Testament. However, many of the people mentioned have dreams and visions, and they did understand them. This indicates that they knew how to do dream interpretation. They already knew how God speaks and did not have to be trained like we do today.

The story in the book of Matthew about the birth of Jesus is full of dreams. Joseph, the husband of Mary, had dreams that were very significant and helped save Jesus' life as a young child.[13] When Jesus was born, the Magi, or wise men, came from faraway lands and were guided to the city where a new King was to be born. They were also warned in a dream to leave Jerusalem after they had found Jesus.[14]

Then later at Jesus' trial, Pontius Pilate's wife had a dream, and she was able to warn her husband to wash his hands of the entire situation.[15] Throughout the book of Acts we see Peter and Paul being guided by dreams and visions. Dreams were a natural part of life in the Bible and need to be a natural part of our lives as well.

Why didn't Jesus interpret dreams?

People ask me all the time why we don't see Jesus interpreting dreams in the Bible. Well, we actually don't know if He interpreted dreams or not. The thing we see Jesus doing the most is teaching and healing people, but there is a verse in the Bible where it says that Jesus did many other things as well. He did so many things that, if they were all written down, the whole world would not be able to contain all the books.[16]

The more important thing to recognize is whether or not interpreting dreams is contrary to any type of biblical principles. As long as we are using the Holy Spirit as our guide and the Bible as a reference, dream interpretation is safe, helpful, and fun.

Secrets of the Kingdom of Heaven

Jesus spoke in parables primarily to reveal to His followers the knowledge of the secrets of the kingdom of heaven.[17] The parables are packed full of powerful life-changing principles and full of symbolism

---

13   Matthew 1:19–21, 2:13, 2:19, 2:22
14   Matthew 2:11–12
15   Matthew 27:18–20
16   John 21:25
17   Matthew 13:10–12

as well. Jesus also said whoever has the knowledge of these principles will be given more. But whoever does not have them, then the little bit they had will be taken from them. This is the condition of people today because many have stopped valuing the supernatural side of God in dreams, parables, and spiritual principles. When we stop valuing this revelation, then we will no longer get it. But the good news is what Jesus said: if you have this knowledge (of parables) you will be given more and you will have an abundance. All you need to do is start placing value on your dreams, reading the parables, and watching for God to speak to you through symbolism, and you will be given more revelation than you can imagine. As we begin to receive more revelation, we must develop our interpretive skills to be able to know what it means and how to apply it to our lives. In the next chapter, we will explore how to recognize symbolic messages in dreams and everyday life.

So what if we see a symbol that is not in the Bible?

Probably one of the most commonly asked questions I get is: "Where is that in the Bible?" When we do not see a symbol clearly defined in the Bible, you can use the process that Jesus did in Mark, Chapter 8. The context of this story is that Jesus and His disciples had just fed 4,000 people miraculously with a few fish and a small amount of bread. And afterwards they had seven basketfuls of bread left over.

Then He left them, got back into the boat, and crossed to the other side. The disciples had forgotten to bring bread, except for one loaf they had with them in the boat. "Be careful," Jesus warned them. "Watch out for the yeast of the Pharisees and that of Herod." They discussed this with one another and said, "It is because we have no bread." Aware of their discussion, Jesus asked them: "Why are you talking about having no bread? Do you still not see or understand? Are your hearts hardened? Do you have eyes but fail to see, and ears but fail to hear?" (Mark 8:13–18)

When Jesus said, "Watch out for the yeast of the Pharisees … " His disciples immediately thought He was speaking literally, so they answered, "Is it because we have no bread?" At that point, Jesus told them that they must have eyes to see and ears to hear. What He was referring to was that they must develop symbolic understanding of things.

Let's break it down more and pretend that this was a dream. Yeast goes into bread, and since the Pharisees were teachers, it is safe to say that the bread represented their teaching. It was like nourishment or spiritual food. But there was something else in their bread or teaching. Symbolically, yeast causes things to rise or puff up. So, the hidden meaning of this small parable was to be careful because the teaching of the Pharisees causes pride. A lesson we can learn is to resist the urge to think literally when things in dreams are often symbolic.

It is interesting that this incident was not even listed as a parable among the commentaries. In fact, none of the commentaries even mention that this was a spiritual lesson on how to develop the ability to think symbolically and understand these hidden messages that God is sending. The Holy Spirit revealed this to me one day when I was reading this section from Mark. And I realized that it is a key to teach people how to understand symbols that we do not see clearly defined. If we do not see a sample clearly defined, then we can do what Jesus suggested and "think like yeast."

Another slice of understanding

Using metaphoric understanding and listening to God, I discovered deeper insight into the rest of this section of Mark.

"When I broke the five loaves for the five thousand, how many basketfuls of pieces did you pick up?" "Twelve," they replied. "And when I broke the seven loaves for the four thousand, how many basketfuls of pieces did you pick up?" They answered, "Seven." He said to them, "Do you still not understand?" (Mark 8:19–20)

Jesus refers to the disciples having twelve and seven baskets of bread left over. At other times Jesus referred to himself as the bread of life. And so symbolically, just as the bread was broken and placed into twelve baskets, so was Jesus later broken by His death on the cross and spiritually placed into the twelve of them.

But what about the seven basketfuls? What did they represent? Again, I could not find this in any commentary. As I researched it more, I got revelation from God that the first level of leadership after Jesus left the earth was the twelve apostles. Then later as they got busy they appointed seven deacons to help them minister to the poor and needy.[18] The seven basketfuls represented the second tier of leadership that was coming. I'm sharing this with you to show you how you can use symbolic thinking as you study the Bible and as you interpret your dreams.

Just as I showed you how symbolism is a very important part of dream interpretation, I also want to get more practical by explaining Common Dreams many have. But first remember, a tree may represent a person or it may represent fruit and life. In order to fully understand we must look at the whole picture. Some symbols will be simpler than others, like the yeast that puffs up and the Pharisees pride; others will take more reflecting and sometimes research.

Common Dreams often get overlooked, yet they can have great meaning when interpreted correctly. I am certain that either you or someone you know has had one of these dreams that are quite common to many. Some of the most common ones are flying, falling, being chased, or even having a baby. Let's take a look at these Common Dreams in the next chapter.

---

18   Acts 6:3

CHAPTER 5

Common Dreams People Have

*It's strange how interesting your dreams are, but when some-
one tries to tell you their dream you're just like "WHATEVER!"*
Comedian Jim Gaffigan

After interpreting thousands of dreams for people, I began to notice patterns. Several dream themes seemed to be common to many people I came in contact with. Dreams like flying, falling, teeth coming loose, running or being chased, having a baby, showing up naked, going to the bathroom in public ... recognize any of these? Chances are you have had one or more of these Common Dreams.

As I give meanings to some of these Common Dreams, realize that I'm generalizing. There may be more details to your dream, but this is the basic meaning for most of them. The following are the most popular Common Dreams. It is important to understand these particular dreams because they may help in the accelerated dream interpretive process.

Baby or pregnant

Both men and women can have this type of dream. Most of the time it is not a literal dream but symbolic. It's talking about birthing something new into your life. It could be a new job, a gift, an anointing, creativity, or even a clever invention.

Below are a few examples of baby or pregnancy dreams.

- *There is more than one baby involved, such as twins or triplets.* This indicates that the new thing coming will be of greater magnitude: double, triple or even quadruple.

- *The baby newly born is soon walking or has a full head of hair and teeth.* This is showing that the new thing coming to you will mature and happen quickly.

- *The baby is not alive or needs to be resuscitated.* This is showing you that there is something that God is trying to do through you but it is being stopped or needs help to get it going again.

- *Someone gives you a baby or you find one.* This indicates that a gift or something new that has been neglected or let go is coming into your hands.

Car or vehicle

Symbolically, cars take you places, so they can represent various aspects of your life—like your job, family, ministry, or calling. Remember to pay attention to the context of the dream and notice who is in the car with you. It could possibly be people from your place of employment, where you attend school, family members, or just you. This can give you clues as to what area of your life the dream pertains to. Look at the condition of the car, the conditions outside the car, where you are going, or if you are lost.

Here are some different kinds of car dreams.

- *The brakes fail, you cannot control the steering, or you are unable to stop.* These say you are going too fast right now or you feel out of control and unable to stop.

- *Your car transforms into a convertible, a racecar, or one of elegance.* This can mean that change is coming to your life—change that will bring greater creativity and impact.

- *Your car gets towed.* There is a calling on your life that you are not fulfilling, and something is trying to take it away from you.

Chased or running

More often than not, dreams that involve running can be frightening. This type of dream usually represents one of two situations. You are either running from something in your life, or you are being chased down by your own destiny and it's trying to catch up with you. Either situation can seem scary because they both require major changes. This type of dream is a strong indication that there's some calling on your life that you have yet to fulfill. Why would something evil try to prevent you from this? It is because you have something great to fulfill in your life for God.

Included here are various kinds of dreams that mimic being chased or running.

- *You suddenly begin to run in slow motion.* This type of dream means that delays are getting in the way of you moving forward. You might want to take an inventory of your life and try to pinpoint what it is.

- *There is a presence of something evil* in your dream. This shows that there is something trying to stop you or work against you. There is no need to be afraid because it shows that you have a high calling on your life. I will show you how to turn these types of dreams around in my chapter on Nightmares.

Deceased relatives

It is not uncommon for deceased relatives to appear in our dreams. Often our parents or grandparents can be symbolic of God giving us advice and guidance. These dreams can also heal grief because of the loss of a loved one. If you have a *recurring theme of deceased relatives from one specific side of the family*, like your mom's side, this can indicate that there is a generational calling on that side of your family that has not yet been fulfilled.

Dying

Although this kind of dream can be frightening, dying in a dream is not always bad. It can be symbolic of leaving one season of your life and moving to an entirely new one. It is possible that the dream is about someone that is going to die, but in most cases, it is symbolic of great change coming.

Example:
A friend dreamed she found her husband dead. A short time after the dream, her husband began to have a spiritual awakening in his life.

Falling

Dreams where you are falling indicate that you are out of control in your life. Falling can also suggest that you may need to let go and take some risk. Most people who have falling dreams also have flying dreams.

If you're having a repeated falling dream, this indicates you need peace in your life. Once the peace manifests, you can get the creative juices flowing and fly again.

The following are a few examples of falling dreams.

- You dream *you are falling and wake up with a jolt.* This shows that God is trying to get your attention and get you to wake up to something new.

- *You slip off a steep ledge or cliff.* This indicates that you are in a time of tight maneuvering and God is encouraging you to hold on.

- *You step off a ledge or high place on your own into a free fall.* This shows that God is calling you to take a risk, or that you are a risk-taker by nature.

Flying

The most popular common dreams are flying dreams. Dreams that involve flying without the use of an airplane are usually very good (depending on context). They indicate you have a high degree of creativity, you have the ability to rise above circumstances, and you are possibly maturing spiritually.

Since flying dreams are the most common, I gave a few more examples so you can see how meanings vary based on context.

- *Trying to take off but failing* can indicate that there is something that you are destined to do but you are experiencing setbacks. It is possible that you are hindering your own advancement, and the dream is letting you know so that you can make the necessary changes.

- *Low/high altitude flight* can show you the level of spiritual maturity you are achieving. If you consistently fly at low altitude, then you will want to examine your life to find ways to grow spiritually. Flying at very high altitude reveals that you are advancing spiritually and that your creativity is increasing.

- *Flying over a known city or region* is usually an indication to pray and intercede for that area, or you may have a connection there.

- *Flight into outer space* is a great dream! This is saying that you are moving or are about to move into high-level spiritual experiences with God.

- *Crashing or out of control* is obvious that your spiritual life needs attention. It may be a warning to bring balance back into your life.

- *Floating or levitating* is similar to flying in that you are rising above situations in your life. Levitation dreams show that God is giving you power to get over some particular situation in your life.

- *Flapping your arms* to fly means that you are using your own efforts instead of God's grace and power in your life.

House

Dreams that take place in and around your home represent some aspect of your life. Notice the context. Are people there from work, school, family, or are they unfamiliar? Watch for clues.

Below are some different kinds of house dreams.

- You go back to your *childhood home even though you are your current age.* This indicates that you are either dealing with family or childhood issues right now, or there is still something to be fulfilled that your ancestors had been called to do.

- You are in a house and *you discover rooms that you never knew existed*. This represents things in your life that you have yet to discover. This could be hidden talents, gifts, or future accomplishments that are available to you.

Late

Showing up late for anything in a dream is a warning to not miss what is coming. It is just making you aware of something approaching. So when you wake up, ask God to help you catch whatever it is.

Losing wallet or purse

When you lose your wallet, purse, or identification, it usually indicates that you are not recognizing your true identity or calling in life.

Lost

This type of dream is showing that you are lacking clear direction. It is possible that you have decisions to make, or that you may need to rethink your plans. This type of dream is another heads-up that you need additional preparation.

Naked

You show up in the dream and realize you forgot to get dressed. Public nakedness is actually a good dream as long as it's not vulgar or pornographic. This type of dream indicates that you are a safe person and people feel free to disclose their problems to you often. When you have this type of dream, watch for people who may need help, or just listen to them. If *you forget one area of clothing,* it may be trying to emphasize a particular type of gifting you have. An example of missing your top or shirt could show you are open and free as you nurture people. If you forget your pants, then you are lacking something that you need for your "walk" or daily life. No shoes can indicate the lack of peace.

Not able to run, move, or speak

Whenever we are unable to run or move in a dream, it indicates that something is trying to stop us or hold us back in life. This interpretation can also be applied to dreams when we are not able to speak or cry out for help. This can indicate there are dark forces working against you, but the good news is that there must be something great for you to fulfill, and that is why you are getting so much resistance.

Past relationship

When you dream about being back in an old relationship again, it usually is symbolic and indicates you may be tempted to go back to old behaviors or an "old lover." Maybe it's a habit of isolating yourself, feeling depressed, overeating, etc. When we have one of these dreams it is a heads-up to be careful. It can also indicate that you are going through something right now that has a connection to that time of your life.

Sexual

Although this might be an uncomfortable topic, many people are having sexual dreams, and not all of them are bad. I'm talking about the ones where you kiss someone but yet it did not necessarily seem intimate or a bad thing. Or, you are in love or married to someone else in the dream even though, in real life, you're not attracted to him or her. In some dreams, you could be lying close, hugging, or holding someone that is not your spouse or partner. These dreams are not always what they appear.

Symbolically, sexual attraction can indicate that you have a similar calling or gifting as that person. You most likely desire, or are drawn to be more intimate with, the spiritual gifts that they have. Again, if you are dealing with things in your life and you have sexual dreams, don't worry that it's something bad in your life. Some sexual dreams may indeed point out the need for deeper healing of coming temptations.

How about those dreams in which you or your spouse or someone you know is having an affair? Don't jump to conclusions! This could simply be symbolic that they are getting too busy with something that is pulling them away emotionally from their relationships. This could be overworking or falling into addictive behaviors. When you have these types of dreams, it is best not to confront the person, but to pray and ask God to bring balance to the person's life.

Teeth

This type of dream reveals you are in need of direction. Teeth chew food and make it useful for the body. Symbolically, teeth chew the word or teaching of God so it can be digested and made useful through application. Chewing or thinking about something brings deeper understanding. That's why teeth coming loose or falling out means you're in need of direction, wisdom, or advice.

Here are examples of various teeth dreams.

- *You bite into some food and your teeth break off.* This indicates that there is something that you are having difficulty understanding at the moment.

- *You look in the mirror* and suddenly your teeth are falling out. You are lacking wisdom in the area of your self-image or who you are and what you're called to do.

- *Your incisor teeth* come loose or fall out. These are also known as "eye teeth" and symbolically, loose incisors can indicate that you are lacking spiritual vision.

- *Your wisdom teeth* come loose or fall out. Obviously, you're lacking wisdom in some area of your life.

- *Your front teeth* come out. This could indicate that you are too busy or "biting off more than you can chew."

Test

When you take a test in a dream, it's giving you an indication that you are in a time of testing with God. To mature, we need to learn life lessons, and God will test us along the way to see if we're ready for advancements and promotions. If *you need to take a test but cannot find the classroom,* then there is some training or preparation you need in order to advance.

Toilet, bathroom, or shower

Dreams situated in bathrooms, toilets, or showers show that something negative needs to be flushed off or cleansed. This does not necessarily mean that it is something major. Things like unforgiveness, anger, and pride to name a few may just need to be flushed. Toilet dreams actually can have a positive outcome.

Below are a few examples of toilet, bathroom, or shower dreams.

- *You cannot find the toilet, or you find one but it is dirty.* This indicates that you have not yet found the type of help that you need to get over some things in your life.

- *If the drain or toilet is plugged up*, then you probably are holding onto something negative, possibly unforgiveness.

- *You need to use the bathroom before leaving to go somewhere.* This shows that you have some things to take care of before moving forward.

- *You find yourself going to the bathroom in public.* This indicates that you are open and vulnerable, and others will help you through this time.

Underwater

Water normally represents spiritual aspects of your life. Being underwater is a great dream because it shows that you are going deeper into spiritual things. When you can breathe underwater, you are maturing.

Weather and disasters

Because we see earthquakes, tornadoes, and tsunamis on the news and they are a part of life, most of the time they are symbolic in dreams. Depending on the context, they can also indicate something of great magnitude or impact coming or times of turmoil. Water often represents the spiritual realm, so a tidal wave can represent a major change coming or movement from God. It is possible that what you are seeing is not symbolic but actually a prophetic warning of a natural disaster coming. Thankfully, it is usually symbolic.

Here are some examples of weather and disaster dreams.

- *A tornado is coming at your house.* You are about to experience turmoil. Usually, if the tornado is white, then God is allowing this to happen.

- *A huge tidal wave is coming and wiping things out.* Something new is coming in the spiritual realm that will wipe out the old and bring in the new.

- *An entire city or area is underwater, flooded.* This could be a move or increase of the Holy Spirit.

We will get into more Common Dream symbols a bit later. For now, begin to notice these dreams. You will want to familiarize yourself with these Common Dreams, as you will see them often. So, whether we are flying or falling, swimming or sinking, we all have Common Dreams! In the next chapter, we will take a look at how to identify the specific purpose of a dream and determine how to respond in ways that will change your life for the good.

CHAPTER 6

Getting the Most Out of a Dream

"A dream which is not interpreted is like a letter which is not read."

(The Talmud)

How do I know what is important?

One of the most important aspects of understanding dreams is simply knowing who or what the dream is about. In my opinion it's probably fifty percent of what you need to know. So many people think that their dreams are about something or someone else when in reality, the dream is often about them. That is why I developed the Four Easy Steps to Dream Interpretation that we went over in Chapter 2. With enough practice using the questions in these steps, you will begin to notice key elements of dreams. Another essential tool is for you to know the purpose of the dream and how to respond to it.

The meaning, purpose, and response

Dream interpretation will become much easier when you learn to separate the meaning of the dream from the purpose or how it essentially applies to your life. These are two totally different things. Most people immediately begin thinking about how the dream applies to their life before giving full consideration to the dream's true interpretation. This rookie mistake is actually why most people don't understand their dreams. To be a really good dream interpreter, sometimes you need to step away from your own thoughts as to what you think it means and take a closer look at the dream itself. You will almost need to remove yourself from the picture so you can get an unbiased view. Let me explain what I mean.

The meaning of the dream is usually very simple. It can normally be stated in a short paragraph and is very persuasive and direct. It is best to state the interpretation of the dream like this: "The meaning of this dream is … " Once you or the dreamer feels that the interpretation is correct, and it feels right, then you can go on to the details of the dream, which is more of its purpose or how it practically applies to your life.

Although there can be more than one meaning, normally there is one main meaning and many applications. The dream can be for you and also symbolic of your job. The dream can be about your family and also apply to others going through the same thing. It will take practice to recognize the three to four main points of the dream because that's where the interpretation lies.

Example:

I dreamed I was with people from my work and I received news that I was pregnant and going to have the baby on March 4th.

The **meaning** of a dream is the bottom line or basic overview of the dream. You can use the Four Steps to Dream Interpretation we have already gone over to get the dream's interpretation. It is usually short and to the point, allowing for a broad application. In this case, the dream is about something new coming regarding your career.

The **purpose** of a dream is to get your attention that something new is coming in your career. In the application, you can go into much more detail on how it practically relates to a situation. "March 4th" is either a date or timing of the new thing or may be a play on words for "march forth," which indicates that you are to move forward boldly. By putting too much emphasis on the application, you may lose the impact of the meaning. If you start trying too hard to figure out what March 4th means, you may forget the exciting news that something new is coming in your life! Another thing to keep in mind is that if you can take a dream symbol out of the dream and it does not dramatically change the meaning, then it's best to not focus on it. If you remove March 4th, the dream does not change all that much.

The **response** is what to do with the meaning of the dream. Responding in some way will make the dream come alive. In the case of this dream, pray and ask God to show you what it is He is bringing in your life and if there is something you can do to help prepare. Various responses for dreams might include: praying, reading, taking a class, calling a friend, doing some research, etc.

Try it on a dream in the Bible

I have gone over four practical steps to understand dreams and what to watch for using "meaning, purpose, and response." Let's try it out on a dream that's already interpreted in the Bible. This really is the true test to see if it works. We'll use the dream of Pharaoh's cupbearer, who lost his job and was in prison at the same time that Joseph, the dream interpreter, was there.

Pharaoh's cupbearer's dream

"So the chief cupbearer told Joseph his dream. He said to him, 'In my dream I saw a vine in front of me, and on the vine were three branches. As soon as it budded, it blossomed, and its clusters ripened into grapes. Pharaoh's cup was in my hand, and I took the grapes, squeezed them into

Pharaoh's cup and put the cup in his hand.'" (Genesis 40:9–11) Let's use my four questions for understanding dreams:

- Who or what is the dream about and what area of life?

- Is the dream positive or negative?

- Are there any repeated themes in the dream or Common Dreams?

- What are the three to four main points of the dream?

You'll notice first of all, the dream is about the cupbearer and has to do with his work. Second, it does seem to be positive. Third, the repeated themes of threes—the three branches and the three stages of the grapes: budding, blossoming, and ripening into clusters. And last, just a few of the main points would be the three branches, three stages, and being back at his job. Now let's look at the interpretation that Joseph gave him.

The meaning

"This is what it means," Joseph said to him. "The three branches are three days. Within three days Pharaoh will lift up your head and restore you to your position, and you will put Pharaoh's cup in his hand, just as you used to do when you were his cupbearer." (Genesis 40:12–13)

Notice how short and to the point Joseph's interpretation is. He correlates the repeated theme or pattern of threes with three days to the fact that the cupbearer had lost his job and was now in prison, and in the dream, he is back on his job. So, you can see that Joseph used a combination of hearing God and symbolism to interpret the dream.

The purpose and response

"But when all goes well with you, remember me and show me kindness; mention me to Pharaoh and get me out of this prison." (Genesis 40:14)

Joseph got the interpretation of the dream, and he responded practically by asking the cupbearer to remember him later so that Joseph could get out of prison. Remember how there could be more than one purpose? One purpose of this dream was to prepare the cupbearer for getting his old job back. Another purpose was to set Joseph up to later step into his life's destiny of interpreting Pharaoh's dream. Then, he not only got released from prison but also was promoted to second in command of all of Egypt. It pays to be a good dream interpreter!

So, you can see that the steps I have outlined and the practical responses work with a dream already interpreted in the Bible. As you develop your ability, your understanding of dreams will get better, and you will soon be able to help people like Joseph did. God is looking for people who can hear His voice, interpret dreams, and step on the scene like Joseph, interpreting dreams even for major world leaders and releasing God's strategies on the earth.

I thought God gave interpretations?

I have trained thousands of dream interpreters, and I still run across people who do not believe that we can learn to interpret our dreams. Many feel that we need to rely 100 percent on revelation from God. This comes partly from Joseph's words as he interpreted the cupbearer's and baker's dreams.

Then Joseph said to them, "Do not interpretations belong to God? Tell me your dreams." (Genesis 40:8)

Yes, we must rely on being guided by the Holy Spirit and listen to God as we interpret a dream, but keep in mind that dreams are also similar to night parables. Jesus taught His followers the need to understand parables by interpreting the meaning. If you study Matthew, Chapter 13, you will see this. It really is okay to practice hearing God in our daily lives. He wants us to hear His voice and know Him better. I will go into more detail on this later.

I am not trying to teach you a method but instead show you how to get to the basic meaning of a dream. Dreams are subjective, and just like parables, symbols may change from dream to dream, so we need to rely on God's revelation to know what each dream means and how to make a practical life application.

How can you tell if a dream is from God, yourself, or other sources?

This is one of the most popular questions I get asked. I will give you a few tips later on how to recognize dreams that are from God or yourself, but the best way to do it is simply practice. The more dreams that you begin to interpret, the better you will get. All God-given gifts, natural talents, or skills must be developed. If you want to be a teacher, you would need to practice. The same goes for a musician or worship leader, administrator, or any other gift or calling. This principle applies to hearing God and dream interpretation as well. The more you do it the better you will get. I'm giving you some tools so that you can get started right away.

Training yourself to look for the main points of the dream will take practice. After you do it a few times, though, it will become automatic, and it will be as though these main points are highlighted and stand out. To become a really good dream interpreter, you will need to train yourself in recognizing these four main points of the dream. As you do that, also learn to recognize the source of the dream and where it is coming from.

PRACTICAL STEPS TO UNDERSTANDING DREAMS

Write your dreams down and save them

It is very important that you value your dreams. You can do this best by writing them down and keeping track of them. Find a recording method that suits your lifestyle and personality. I used to write my dreams in a paper dream journal. My journals date back over twenty years, and I have them stored in boxes. The problem for me is that I am an avid dreamer, so when I tried to find a dream I had previously, I needed to search through a pile of dream journals over four feet high. Over ten years ago, I converted to a computer dream journal. At first it was awkward because I was so used to writing things down with pen and paper, but now, I wouldn't do it any other way. I go into much more detail. I can cross-reference them and do searches. The most important thing is to track how your dreams are fulfilled.

Pray for divine understanding

Even though I am giving you steps to understand your dreams, remember that we must rely on hearing God as well as learn to understand symbolism. So the very first thing to do is pray and ask God to speak to you about the meaning of the dream. We can never get away from relying on the Holy Spirit to guide us. You might hear me repeat this because it is a really important part of interpreting dreams.

Make notes and do research

If you are using the steps that I recommend for understanding dreams, things will become clearer because you'll know what to focus on in the dream. There will still be things that you may not understand, and you will need to research. I have used reference material like a book on the meaning of names, biblical imagery, and some dream symbols books. I now primarily use an Internet search engine. I have a bibliography at the end of this book with reference materials that can help you. Another important aspect of recording and journaling your dreams is that you can go back later and update them with notes and details. The more notes you take, the more understanding you will develop. You really do get out of it what you put into it.

Constellation Orion the Hunter dream

Let me give you an example of researching a dream. I had a dream that I was standing, looking at the night sky, and I saw the constellation Orion the Hunter rising in the East. I did an Internet search and found that Orion the Hunter rises in the east during the harvest time. This brought greater understanding that my dream was about something new that was about to happen that was currently hidden that would eventually produce a great result or yield a harvest.

Follow through on direction you receive

One of the major principles of understanding how God speaks in dreams and in everyday life is to follow through on any revelation or direction that we receive. If you are not valuing how God speaks to you, then you may not receive additional revelation. Following through could include practical steps such as making a phone call, sending an email, forgiving someone, etc.

Study the dreams and parables in the Bible

It is really important to frequently study symbolic language such as parables and dreams in the Bible. Commit yourself to continual learning, and keep your gifts sharpened by regularly using them. After interpreting dreams for over twenty years, I still do this. Whenever I have spare time or don't know what to read in the Bible, I read parables, psalms, or dreams like in the book of Daniel. It's funny because I've been studying these for years and yet I still notice new things. Make it easy for yourself by carrying the Bible on your smart phone or pulling it up on your computer.

We must consider dream interpretation and hearing God like any other gift that God can give us. The more we use it, the better we get.[19] But if we do not use it, we will eventually become dulled to it. You can train yourself daily as if you are a professional athlete or singer. This is

---

19   Hebrews 5:14

what will set apart those who can develop accurately in dream interpretation. You can start out small and grow over time. Consistency is the key.

There is no way around the fact that dream interpretation takes a lot of practice. The more dreams you interpret, the better you will get. You may feel somewhat confused and lack confidence at first, but don't give up; stick with the process, because a light will come on the more you do it. It is also good to interpret dreams other than your own. Your own dreams are harder to understand because we try to apply them before we interpret them.

Dreams can seem crazy and chaotic, but after you learn what to look for, you can get something out of nearly every dream that can be practically applied to your life. Interpreting dreams has evolved over the years to what some consider an art form. One amazing way to understand symbolic language is through the arts. Let's take a look at metaphoric messages in movies.

CHAPTER 7

Develop Metaphoric Thinking

*"Last night I dreamed I ate a ten-pound marshmallow
and when I woke up the pillow was gone."*

Tommy Cooper

It can be very intriguing when you figure out a dream's hidden message; it's almost like decoding a secret from God, like you are His agent. There's nothing better than seeing the twinkle of "ah-ha" in a dreamer's eye whenever your interpretation hits it right! I mentioned previously that you cannot interpret a dream accurately by using a list of symbols. It is necessary to learn to think metaphorically or symbolically if you want to become a really good dream interpreter. Understanding metaphors is essential because the more you get into dreams, the more you will see various dream metaphor examples from different people and different places.

What is a metaphor?

A *metaphor* is a figure of speech where one thing is expressed in terms of another. A metaphor can be a visual representation, that is, a symbol.

For example, "a sea of troubles." If I just said I'm going through a difficult time, it does not express the depth of it. A metaphor can richly describe a situation visually. I use the terms metaphor and symbol interchangeably throughout this book, just so you know, these are very close in meaning.

In addition, a *simile* is a figure of speech using words such as *like* or *as* to compare two things. An example of a simile would be: Alex is "strong *as* an ox." People use metaphors and similes all the time to compare one thing to another and may not even realize it. They are part of our everyday speech.

Easy way to understand metaphors

Here's the easiest way to think metaphorically: think of something in nature and what it does. Let's use the metaphor of animals. A bird flying high in the air represents the ability to achieve things on a higher level. Butterflies go through a major transformational process, which is symbolic of going through a difficult time and emerging beautiful. Fish swim in water with water representing the spiritual aspect of life. Some fish can be symbolic of the ability to be spiritually attuned, but sharks can represent a vicious attack (verbally or emotionally).

Here are some more examples in nature. Rats and mice are drawn to garbage and can simply indicate the presence of something negative in your life that needs to be cleaned up. Horses have power. Donkeys can be stubborn. Dogs are man's best friend. Cats tend to be more independent.

All these characteristics of animals can be symbolic of other things in real life. When you learn to recognize the function or characteristic of something, and in our case apply it to dreams, you'll understand the metaphor's meaning.

Learn to think metaphorically

Life is full of metaphors. Begin to look for hidden messages in things that you see in your daily life. Notice street signs, songs on the radio or in stores, commercials, billboards, addresses, and numbers. Not everything will be God speaking to you, but quite often you can recognize God's voice in metaphors in your daily life. When we learn to decipher metaphors, we can gain deeper meaning into life. My entire life is like a parable, and things that have happened to me are often hidden messages from God.

Just take a fresh look around and ask yourself, "If this were happening in a dream, what would it mean?" For example, a friend picked me up at an airport, and we had a one and a half hour drive to my hotel. An hour into the trip, we realized that he had driven the wrong way. This was a prophetic message that in making decisions, he had to be careful not to go the wrong way. Unfortunately, a short time later, he did end up going in a wrong way that was quite costly to his organization.

Watch for repeating metaphors … repeating metaphors … repeating metaphors …

I went through a time in which lights were repeatedly burning out in my house and in my cars. I would replace the bulbs, and they would burn out again within weeks. Most people would think that I was burned out, but I knew God was giving me a heads up to *not* get burned out. And so my response was to take some time off.

My wife and I pay attention to repeating numbers all the time. Eleven can represent transition and we know that we're about to transition into an entirely new season of our lives. Maybe you see numbers line up on the clock like 2:22, 3:33, etc. It could be the meaning of the actual number or symbolic that things are about to line up for you. The only way to know for sure is to record it, watch for it, and ask God for confirmation.

Metaphoric exercises

Here's a fun and helpful exercise you can do to understand metaphors. Take a moment right now and think of a person you know, and describe them as an animal. Be nice, of course. Maybe it's their appearance or an aspect of their personality that causes you to choose one animal over another.

Next, describe what they do (or their career) as a boat. What kind of boat would they have? Are they like a sailboat, gently coasting by the wind of the Spirit? Or are they more like a speedboat that can bolt quickly and have fun? Are they more like an aircraft carrier supporting other people, or a mercy ship because of their compassion? People describe me as a cruise ship because of my sense of humor.

Metaphors in movies

Remember that Jesus often taught deep spiritual principles by using simple, symbolic examples from everyday life. I believe that if Jesus were teaching today, He would use movies or television to creatively explain valuable truths by parables. People are familiar with today's movies and television, but some people are not aware of the hidden meanings in the shows right before their eyes. Let's take a look at some metaphors in movies.

Superhero movies

Most superhero movies have the same type of theme. They feature supernaturally gifted people who use their powers to help people and fight evil, but when they stop using their supernatural abilities, crime and evil tend to increase. This is symbolic of when Christians stop using their God-given supernatural gifts. It is as if evil increases. But just like in the movies, when they go back to using their supernatural powers, the world seems to balance out again.

The Incredibles

A really helpful example to understanding metaphors is the animated movie *The Incredibles*. It is about The Parr family, who possess supernatural powers.[20] There were five family members, which is symbolic of the fivefold ministry gifts that are mentioned in the Bible.[21] The father had supernatural strength, but sometimes he was too strong and would break things. This is a metaphor for people who become too spiritual and rigid and lack grace. They inadvertently end up breaking a lot of things and hurting people around them. The dad needed balance, and he had that in his wife, whose supernatural power was flexibility. Strength requires flexibility or we end up hurting people.

Most people thought the daughter Violet's supernatural gifting was the ability to disappear, but actually, she wanted to disappear because she didn't want anyone to see her. Later, she discovered that her true supernatural ability was to cover her family with the bubble of protection—a force field. This is symbolic of having the gift of prayer and intercession. When she discovered her true gift, she no longer wanted to disappear. Instead, she became very interactive with her friends. Wanting to disappear is a metaphor for people who are supernaturally gifted by God but don't want anyone to know about it. This is called false humility, and there are many "Violets" out there who need to discover their true identity in God.

And then there was their son named Dash, whose ability was to move very quickly. This is symbolic of our need to move quickly in making decisions and getting things done. And then there was the baby, Jack-Jack. Most people may have thought that Jack-Jack might have been evil because of his appearance, but actually, he could do everything that all the other family members could do all at once. He was the most gifted in the entire family yet he was just an infant. This is symbolic of a generation that is rising up right now that is so very talented but not yet matured in their gifts and callings. They are breaking many records in sports without the use of steroids and setting new standards.

Another character was the young family friend named Buddy. He was not a family member but he came to Mr. Parr and asked to be mentored. But the dad had no time for him and told him to leave, so Buddy went off and built a machine that allowed him to do supernatural

---

20   Original concept by Jeannine Rodriguez, Images of Light Ministries
21   Ephesians 4:11

things. It was more of a counterfeit than an actual supernatural gift. This is symbolic of people who have come to us to be trained in the things of God but we've sent them away because they didn't fit into our family mold. Many of these highly gifted people have come to churches or even approached us, but we turn them away because we did not understand them. They went off discouraged never to come near God or a church again. Some of them were so gifted that they developed groups such as the human potential movement and the New Age that are using biblical principles without a personal relationship with God or the power of the Holy Spirit. When I say this, I am not being judgmental because I was once one of those highly gifted people who came to the church but was turned away.

Spider-Man, Spider-Man 2, Spider-Man 3

Like other superhero movies, *Spider-Man* is a classic example to study to learn how to think metaphorically. Spider-Man's name was Peter and he was very much in love with Mary, but Mary loved another man who was very evil. Mary can represent the church today and Peter can represent those who are following God's plan for their life. God is so in love with the church but the church is in love with the world (the evil man). Think of the symbolism of a spider. Spiders seem negative, but Spider-Man was actually very positive and cared about people. This is very similar to Christians who understand and operate in the supernatural power of God. They seem evil or even negative to others but in reality they are not (well, most of them). When Spider-Man stopped using his powers, he lost vision, had to use glasses to see, and crime began to increase around him.

In *Spider-Man 3* he got black stuff all over him, which was pride. And in the movie he had to go to a church to get the pride off of him. This was not even a Christian movie, yet it was prophetic and has many more layers of symbolic meaning.

Inception

The movie *Inception* was all about the world of dreams. They did a great job with special effects, capturing what a dream looks and feels like, but there was a lot of symbolism in that movie as well. The symbolic meaning is that there is an evil force in the world trying to steal the dreams of people. It revealed that some people have the ability to use dreams to go into deep areas within ourselves and unlock the fears that are holding us back from our future.

Avatar

The symbolic meaning behind *Avatar* is that there is a negative force that we don't understand that's trying to destroy people. Avatar bodies are like the supernatural abilities that we can have in God. The evil force was driven by greed. We need to step into our supernatural abilities, (or our avatar bodies), to be all God has called us to be and change the world for good.

Dark Knight Rises and The Amazing Spider-Man

Batman and Spiderman are great metaphoric pictures of how God will take something that looks bad or intended for evil and use it for good. Bats and spiders may not seem positive, but Batman and Spider-Man are very positive as they fight evil and restore justice. This is a prophetic picture of the spiritual warfare that is going on all the time.

In *The Amazing Spider-Man*, a gas was released that turns people into lizards. This symbolizes a Satanic attack right now to get people to become coldblooded and lack the ability to love. This is happening in people today as a mean spirit has entered our society. It is interesting that Batman and Spider-Man could not take the enemy down by themselves but had to operate as a team with others. This is a message for us today that God is calling us to work together in greater unity and there will not be many Lone Rangers.

Now that we have seen modern day examples of metaphors in the media, let's try interpreting metaphors with an example of a vision in the Bible. Dreams and visions are closely related, so deciphering metaphors from a dream is very similar to doing so with a vision. Please note that any dream or vision that is literal (what you see is what you get) or actually happens does not need an interpretation. Whenever you see things that are symbolic in a dream or a vision, then it requires interpretation.

Peter's trance

The Bible describes when Peter had a vision while he was in a trance in Acts: "He saw heaven opened and something like a large sheet being let down to earth by its four corners. It contained all kinds of four-footed animals, as well as reptiles and birds. Then a voice told him, 'Get up, Peter. Kill and eat.' 'Surely not, Lord!' Peter replied. 'I have never eaten anything impure or unclean.' The voice spoke to him a second time, 'Do not call anything impure that God has made clean.' " (Acts 10:11–15)

Let's look more closely at the symbol of the animals in Peter's vision in Acts 10:12. When Peter sees the unclean animals that were not to be eaten by Jews,[22] he could have easily misunderstood this metaphor to mean God was speaking about his diet or the farmer nearby. However, a few moments later, a group of non-Jewish people came looking for Peter because an angel had told them Peter's name and where he would be staying. This was a major confirmation, which supported the meaning behind the vision that Peter received. When God speaks to us, especially in dreams and visions, He will often confirm it in some other way, and there will be context for how it applies.

God was communicating to Peter through symbolism that he must take the message of Jesus to the non-Jewish people. This rocked Peter's theology because the belief system of his day said that salvation could only come to the Jewish people. So, when God wanted to expand Peter's understanding of His love for the entire world, He spoke to Peter with a symbolic message in a vision.

22   See Leviticus 11 and Deuteronomy 14

You will begin to see metaphors and symbolic messages in the world around you. As you begin to plunge into stories like the one above concerning Peter, more symbols will register for you in the Bible. You'll start to notice them even more after reading this book. Spider-Man, Batman, and even the darker movies I mentioned all have metaphors. Cartoons and even the name of the street you live on can have a symbolic message. As you draw your attention to something, your brain will automatically start highlighting it for you to investigate. To help you understand this, let's now go deeper and look at how the meaning of a symbol or metaphor can change based on context.

CHAPTER 8

Context Makes a Difference

"I dream my painting and I paint my dream."
Vincent van Gogh

I mentioned that my life is a continuous parable. I see metaphoric messages nearly every day, and they seem to appear everywhere I go. God is speaking to all of us this way, but most people have not tuned into it or noticed. My desire is to teach you these tools so you can be more aware of how God used symbols throughout the Bible to speak to people and that He hasn't stopped now. Let me give you some examples!

Parable of the sixes

I travel a lot and speak at many conferences, and often the things that happen to me on the way to a particular event symbolize a real life parable for that group or city. I was going to speak at a church in Canada. On the way out the door, my wife handed me $6 of Canadian coins that she had found. When I got to the airport, I was in seat 6 on both flights and I arrived at gate 66. They picked me up and took me to Motel 6. Wow, with all those sixes, most people would think it was negative (666). But as I was talking to some of the leaders from the church, they mentioned to me something that had happened six years ago. God gave me the understanding of it: they had started something six years ago that had gotten off track, and they needed to go back to that original vision.

People can misunderstand these cloaked messages from God when they have not grasped both the language of symbolism and how it functions with metaphors. When you practice placing your attention on it, thinking metaphorically becomes easier and even automatic so that eventually, you will not have to ponder what all the symbols mean in a dream, vision, or real life parable. It will become automatic and you will just know what God is saying.

In this chapter, we look at why something like the number six might seem negative to some yet could be used positively. We will take a look at why symbols and metaphors can change from dream to dream.

Symbols can change

Now that you understand how metaphors work, let me add in a new level of understanding for you. The meaning of metaphors and symbols can change based on how they appear or how they are functioning. Although there are plenty of common metaphors, we have to be careful not to interpret the same symbol the same way for every dream. I do generalize some of the Common Dream themes that we will go over shortly, but even those can change based on the context in which they appear.

You may have heard the saying, "A picture is worth a thousand words." This accurately describes the world of metaphors in dreams. One symbol might represent many different things. For example, if you see a certain person in a dream, it is possible they represent something other than themselves. Maybe it is the meaning of their name, possibly their position in life, or what they are doing that sheds deeper light on the dream's meaning.

Even Jesus changed a symbol's meaning

When Jesus spoke in parables, He taught deep spiritual principles by comparing them to common things in everyday life. It was as if He was saying, "Picture this … this is what the Kingdom of Heaven is like." Jesus made reference to "seeds" several times. Once, He compared seeds to having faith, another time, He compared seeds to the word of God, and still another time, to spreading the good news.[23] The meaning of the symbol "seed" changed from parable to parable based on the context.

Just like Jesus' symbols in His parables, dream symbols can change from one dream to another. This is why we need to be careful that we understand how the metaphor is used within the dream—the context in which it is being presented. So, if a metaphor or symbol changes, how do we figure out what it means? Context is key.

Understanding symbols in context

The context of the symbol is what really counts because it tells us what it applies to and how. The context helps us understand if the dream is positive or negative, giving us a lot of clues about what area of our lives the metaphor applies to. Context can tell us if it is about ourselves or someone else, or if it's about our personal life or work life.

In my opinion, learning to recognize context is one of the most important things about understanding dreams. When you get the symbol's context, you will know how to apply the dream practically, which will help change your life in some way. So, we need a combination of symbolic understanding and recognizing the context of how the dream symbol appears.

Let's take the color blue. Is it the beautiful hue of periwinkle blue in the flower in your love's flowing brown hair, or is it the blue in the eye of the dinosaur about to eat you? That's context! So when someone asks me a question like, "What does the color blue mean?" I ask a quick question to confirm if it is positive or negative. Remember that in step

23   Matthew 17:20, Luke 8:11, Matthew 13

two of the Four Steps to Understanding Dreams, you ask yourself if the dream is positive or negative. You will also need to ask yourself this when evaluating a particular symbol.

President comes to my house dream

It was right around election time a few years ago, and a friend of mine had a dream that she was having people over to her house and lots of activity was happening. Then, at the end of the dream, the President dropped by for a visit. She was alarmed that the dream indicated that she was supposed to vote for the re-election of the President even though she did not feel that it was the right thing to do. The context of the dream was showing that it was about her life, and something that was going to happen at her house. Because the President is symbolic of authority, it indicated that new authority was coming to her. Sure enough, she had recently made a decision to have a small group of women meet at her house. The context of the dream was not about voting for the President but was confirmation that God was giving her new authority or blessing for the group starting at her house.

You get the idea that the symbols of the dream can change based on what they are doing. It's more like how they are functioning and what the end result is. That's the danger of using symbols without context. You need to know context in order to figure out the symbolism.

Understanding metaphors in context

Let's take a look at some examples of typical dream metaphors in context. The more you see them, the more you will understand. Please keep in mind it takes practice. Even as a dream expert I still keep my gift sharp by practicing daily. Since I am thin I often joke that "spiritually, I am buff." It is because I work out by going to the metaphor gym every day. Let's do a few metaphoric workouts right now.

I want to show you these examples so that you can learn to recognize symbols in context. To make these concepts easier to differentiate I italicized *the metaphor's meaning* and underlined the context.

The metaphor of playing chess in a dream can represent *strategic moves in your life*. But playing chess <u>in the dark</u> indicates that you lack ability to see your next move. Note how the context here gives added instruction.

Getting a new high-tech cell phone can indicate that you are *advancing in your ability to communicate*. But buying a high-tech cell phone <u>from a drug dealer</u> can be a warning not to make a shady deal, and to be honest.

The brakes going out on your car means that you are in a time where *you feel out of control or in a difficult time*. However, the brakes going out on your car and <u>your car flying away</u> suddenly means that it is a difficult time but you will overcome it.

Evil men or thugs trying to beat you up indicate that there is *spiritual warfare coming against you*. But if you're able to suddenly <u>make some amazing self-defense moves and take out a whole crowd of them</u>, then you are overcoming this attack.

Driving a brand new car can be a *new opportunity coming*. However, if the car turns into a <u>"Fred Flintstone" car and you are using your feet</u>, then you are using your own efforts and not tapping into God's strength.

Making a telephone call to a friend can mean that you are *attempting to vocalize something*. But if your <u>phone keeps going dead</u>, it means that something is trying to cut off the communication between you and another person.

Ordering something to drink or eat means *there is something you need, like information or revelation, that will help you*. But <u>if no one can understand you when you try to order</u>, then something is trying to stop this process. It is really important to pay attention to dreams where something is trying to stop you. This is a sure indicator that you are about to have a breakthrough in your life if you are persistent. Please don't give up.

Looking around in a dream means that you need to *pay attention to your present situation*. If you are <u>unable to see clearly</u>, then the context indicates this is a time in your life when things are not clear. Cloudy vision can clear up by getting more focused and asking God to reveal a strategy on what to do next.

Being given a book and map means that you are *getting strategies or revelation*. If you are given a book or map <u>by a faceless person</u>, faceless people can represent angels sent by God, so this means you are getting the strategy directly from Heaven.

You dream that you are going into a bright white closet. Closets represent a few different things (like *hiding, prayer, something very personal*). That is why we have to note the context. A <u>bright white closet </u>would most likely indicate God calling you into a time of prayer and intimacy.

Driving your car is a metaphor for *being able to go forward in your life*. If you are driving <u>in the rain and then it clears up</u>, then this indicates you are in a time that was once unclear but things are shifting and the season is changing. If your car is going <u>in reverse</u>, then you are moving away from your destiny right now.

Swimming in water can represent the *spiritual aspect of life*. So, swimming can be good, but notice the context of the water: is it <u>clear or dirty, fast-flowing or stagnant, or is it shallow or deep</u>? The context of how you are swimming in water will help you understand more about what is happening with your spiritual life. If you are swimming in <u>clear</u> water this means that your spiritual life is refreshing and life-producing. Swimming in <u>dirty</u> water indicates that some issues might need to be addressed or healed. If you are swimming in <u>fast-flowing</u> water, get ready for things to accelerate and get real exciting. Swimming in <u>stagnant</u> water indicates that you may be stuck and need to start moving again. If the water is <u>shallow</u>, this indicates that you might be too comfortable and need a challenge. Swimming in <u>deep</u> water shows that you are maturing spiritually and possibly taking more risks.

Running in <u>slow motion</u> means that this is either *a time when things are slowing down*, or *something is trying to keep you from moving quickly*. Take positive action by checking your life to see if there is something that you are doing that is slowing you down. Positive action may help free you up.

Time traveling means that you are *impacting other areas of life*. If you time travel <u>to the future</u>, this can indicate that you are in a time of acceleration. If you time travel <u>to the past</u>, then there is something from the past that needs to be taken care of or dealt with.

You wearing shoes with different colors indicates your *destiny or things that you are called to walk in*. They can also be symbolic of peace. It is very important to notice if <u>your shoes are on or off</u> because it shows if you are gaining or lacking. Sometimes, the colors may add more meaning, but most of the time the shoes are the main point.

Giving gifts <u>freely</u> to people: this is either a calling for you to *help other people*, or you have the *special ability to impart spiritual gifts to other people*. Either way, it shows that you are a giver and a person of compassion.

Planting/gardening could be symbolic that you are in a *time of growth and starting new things*. If <u>gardening is a hobby</u> for you, then this may be telling you to spend more time in your garden.

Fishing can symbolically mean there are *things in the spirit that you need*. It may also be that you have a *destiny on your life to help other people*. Jesus told His three closest disciples: Peter, James, and John—who were fishermen—that He would make them "fishers of men."[24] If <u>fishing is leisure for you</u>, then this type of dream is calling you to more recreation.

Why a symbols list doesn't work

I think now you get it. A symbol in a dream can change the meaning based on its context. You cannot use only a list of symbols to accurately interpret a dream, as you now see. Knowing some basic symbols is necessary at first, but understanding their functional use in a dream allows you to go much deeper. That does not mean that you cannot use symbols lists as a basic guideline, but relying on the list as your primary means of interpreting dreams will limit your interpretations, and they will often turn out with a generic or half-baked sound to them. When I was a new dream interpreter, I did this often, and I noticed that my dream interpretations were shallow and did not have impact. After learning to recognize the main points of a dream and the context of the symbols, my dream interpretation went to a new level that brought more impact to others and even to me.

---

24   Matthew 4:19 New King James Version

Find metaphors in your life

Be aware that each of us has a personal dream or symbolic language based on our culture, background, and beliefs. Begin to notice repeated symbols or themes that are appearing in your dreams or life. It could very well be that God is trying to communicate something to you. You may want to write them in a journal so that you can track them. Also notice the context in which they appear. Do you have more repeated themes about your family, work, or your spiritual life? These are clues that will allow you to know what area of your life to work on or improve. This allows you to work hand-in-hand with God as He draws you closer to your destiny. After studying dreams, I determined that there are many dreams that we have at night that can point us to our life dreams. In the next chapter, we will look at various types of dreams and their functions so you will know how to respond with greater purpose.

CHAPTER 9

Purpose to the Mystery

"The most beautiful thing we can experience is the mysterious. It is the source of all true art and science."

Albert Einstein

Knowing the source of dreams

The most commonly asked question I get about dreams is, "How do I know if a dream is from God or not?" The answer is not easily explained, as it takes practice. I often use the analogy of someone who is an expert at identifying anything that is a counterfeit. They would have to first study the real thing before they are conditioned to quickly identify a fake. Dreams are similar, and as you study and take notes in your dream journal you will more easily notice dream sources. You can have a dream from yourself, which is from your own desires, or a dream that reveals the plans of darkness against you. These tend to be dull-colored dreams or even black and white.

Dreams from God usually have more color and a positive feel to them. However, as we go into nightmares, we will see that there actually is a nightmare in the Bible that was given to a king by God to try to get him to change. So, it is a bit tricky at first to identify if a dream is from God or not. It will take practice, and as you will find in this book, God can use just about any dream you have to change your life.

Types of dreams and their functions

Understanding dreams cannot be put in a box. Not all dreams are the same, and many people attribute a strange dream to something they may have eaten or watched on T.V. Once you begin to recognize various dreams, you will see that each one can have a specific purpose. Some dreams provide you with insight into yourself and are a means for self-exploration. Other dreams may be prophetic in nature, and some can be an avenue of healing. Dreams may even reveal your life calling or destiny. In this chapter, we will discover various types of dreams and their purpose.

Destiny and calling

There are several types of dreams that you may want to particularly be aware of. These are the ones that pertain to your destiny or life calling. Some of these destiny dreams actually reveal a future career or higher calling you may be invited to fulfill.

After interpreting thousands of dreams for people, I began to notice a common pattern. There are some dreams that people seem to have that indicate that there is something more for them to fulfill in their lives. I have seen so many dreams about people's destiny that I became a Life Coach as well as a dream interpreter. There are so many people who are living their lives without clear direction. They are often surprised to find that a night dream they thought was insignificant was holding some major keys that could unlock their destiny.

Some destiny dreams may first appear to be negative, such as nightmares or those involving running or being chased. There must be something great about to happen in your life if something negative or evil is trying to stop you. Other destiny dreams can include taking a test, showing up late, being naked, teeth coming loose or falling out, or being pregnant or having a baby. I will go into the details of these dreams later in the Common Dreams section.

Revealing your fears

If we have fear in our lives, it holds us back from maturing and advancing. Fear of rejection, fear of failure, fear of success, fear of being alone, fear of love, fear of the unknown—whatever it might be for you, it boils down to not being good for you. The words "do not be afraid" appear in the Bible nearly seventy times. Fear dreams usually involve feeling trapped or feeling unable to move, see clearly, or speak out, to name a few. They may also reveal something positive that God is calling us to, but they also highlight the fear that is holding us back.

Years ago I was about to make a significant career change. I had heard God very clearly and had lots of revelation and confirmation from people around me. Then, the night after I made the decision to take the job, I had a dream that the president of the company I was going to work for was angry and disgusted with me. I woke up wondering if I had made a mistake with my decision. I realized that I had a load of confirmation dreams and prophetic words to do it, and so this one dream seemed out of place. It was from my own fears. I broke through my fear of failure and it was a turning point in my career.

Healing

You can actually get healed emotionally or physically in a dream. Watch for dreams of cleansing, flushing, or being showered off. Some of these dreams may take place in the context of a bathroom or shower.

A woman had a dream just after her husband died. He was in a great place and he came to her to reassure her that he was fine. This dream healed her of grief, and she was able to get on with her life. You can also have a dream that you get physically healed and wake up feeling great. It is important to recognize that our waking life and dream life are closely related.

Interactive or lucid

Any dream in which you know you are dreaming or you are able to do something to change the direction of the dream is called lucid dreaming. An example of this would be the ability to wake yourself up from a bad dream or fly away from something that is attacking you. It can also be positive when you learn to stay asleep and interact with the dream. For instance, you have a recurring dream that there is a door that is locked, and in the dream, you find a way to unlock the door. This is important when it comes to dealing with recurring dreams or nightmares. You can change the outcome. When you change your dream life, know that you are also changing your waking life as well.

Nightmares

It does not take a dream expert to tell you what a nightmare is like. They are usually dark, muted, black and white, and have the feeling of a lot of fear or evil. When we have nightmares or anything negative, it is not usually God's will for our life. These types of dreams are showing us that something wants to hold us back from all the good things that God has for us. Since these types of dreams show Satan's will and not God's will, we need to flip them around and begin to pray the opposite will happen. The only true reality for you is God's intention. We will go into nightmares in more detail later in the book.

Physical or environmental

Sometimes people attribute a strange dream to something they ate. It is possible that what we eat can affect our dreams, but I have found that there are fewer of these dreams than people realize. Medication, alcohol, reaction to food or our environment can indeed affect our dreams. Most people are not trained enough to discern the difference between these various dreams. If you eat a heavy meal too late, you might dream you are being chased by a giant meatball.

It is also possible that you might be picking up on something happening in the spiritual environment around you. People who have a spiritual gift of discerning of spirits often have dreams of demonic attacks that might be coming against people in your close proximity.

Prayer strategy

You can have a dream that will reveal deeper insight about a person or situation. Most of these dreams are given to you to let you know how you can privately pray and support others. Knowing when to actually share them with the person or people involved takes practice. Pray, asking God to let you know, and notice how the people respond.

Someone had a dream that I was crying and really distressed. They contacted me, and yes indeed I was going through a difficult time. I appreciated knowing God knew about my pain and that someone was praying for me.

When I have dreams that reveal people's difficulties or struggles, I simply wake up and pray for them. Sometimes I feel it would be helpful to actually contact them, but prayer itself can often change the person more than confronting them. I say that my preferred method of receiving correction is in a dream. Wouldn't you?

Recurring

Any recurring dream is an indication that God wants to either do something new in your life or is drawing your attention so that you change something. Once you either establish the new behavior or take care of the issue, then these recurring dreams will stop. Most recurring dreams have the same type of theme like running, falling, or being unable to move or speak. The most common recurring dream is being chased by something evil. We really need to pay close attention to recurring dreams as they can reveal our future and any obstacles holding us back.

Spiritual warfare

Dreams where we are battling, defending ourselves, or fighting can indicate that we are in a time of spiritual warfare. Though they may be exhausting, fearful, and even disconcerting, spiritual warfare dreams will free us up spiritually. When we battle in a dream we will experience advancement in our waking life. Warring dreams may involve hand-to-hand combat, swords, guns, knives, bows and arrows, and the like. If these dreams persist you may want to consult a friend or family member to pray with you. It is also possible that you have a spiritual warfare intercession gift in which you battle for other people.

Spiritual experiences

Dreams are not always just a vision in the night. Sometimes a spiritual experience can be mistaken for a dream. The apostle Peter had an experience in which an angel of God came and literally broke him out of jail, and he thought it was a vision or a dream.[25] Dreams, visions, and spiritual experiences all go hand in hand with the supernatural. When we enter a dream, we are literally in the spiritual realm.

I have had my share of spiritual experiences that seemed like dreams. The reason I knew it was more than a dream is that when I woke from it, I was given knowledge of people and taken to places that I have never been. The next day, I went to the place I saw in the experience and actually met the people, and it was just as I saw in the experience. Not all dreams of this nature are actual spiritual experiences, but it is good to be aware that this type of thing can actually happen.

---

25   Acts 12:9

Warning dreams

Dreams can give us a "heads-up" to things that are coming or could potentially happen if we don't take action. They are not always reality, and it's not always set in stone that the dream is exactly what will happen. Warning dreams can guide us to be careful that we make good decisions. Some warning dreams can tell us exactly what will take place. I had a dream that a family member got in a major car accident. I prayed, and while the accident did indeed occur, it was minor and there were no injuries. So, the warning dream was also prophetic and intercessory as well.

About ourselves or about others

Within the dream categories I just mentioned, you could have dreams about yourself or about others. Learning to determine the difference between the two will be very helpful because you will then know how to properly respond.

Most people's dreams are primarily about themselves and the various aspects of their lives. But we are all wired differently, so some people have more dreams for others than they do for themselves. When you have the dream, the best place to start to understand it is to first consider if the dream is revealing anything in your own life before jumping to conclusions about other people. Symbolism can be quite tricky, so we need to be careful when considering whether the dream might be about someone else. Dreams about ourselves can be very revealing and even healing once we learn to recognize them.

Literal or symbolic dreaming

Some people dream literally—that is, what you see is what you get. It is usually a small percentage of people who dream this way. In fact, if you are a literal dreamer, then it does not take a lot of effort to understand your dreams. You will, however, need to learn more about application and how to respond to each dream.

If you are like most people, you dream symbolically. That means that there are things in your dreams that are out of proportion or not normal in everyday life. For example, you might be flying a helicopter down the hallway of your home. We know in real life this is not possible, so that makes it symbolic, and we will need to use metaphoric understanding to decipher the message in the dream.

Most of my dreams are symbolic, but I occasionally have literal dreams, when what I see in the dream comes to pass in real life. I've talked to a lot of people who have told me that they dream about things and then see them happen, and it scares them. It's really important to not be afraid of things like this. You may have a gift to know things in advance, and unless God speaks to you about it, there is no pressure for you to respond.

So, it really makes no difference whether you dream symbolically or literally about yourself or about other people. What we all have in common is this wonderful and wild world of night dreams that fascinate us all.

The list of "dream types" I just presented is fairly basic, but it gives you enough information to begin understanding your dreams now. I have found that these are the ones we see most often. A single dream might also fall into more than one category. It can be a spiritual warfare dream that is warning you about something and giving you a strategy in which to pray. Prayer can change or prevent what is coming, and you can wake up with a new outlook on your situation.

We have covered a lot so far. Now it's time to take a look at some dream symbols. As we do this, keep in mind that symbols may change from dream to dream, and you will be a more effective dream interpreter if you learn to think metaphorically and recognize the context in which symbols appear.

CHAPTER 10

Dream Symbols

"Dreams say what they mean, but they don't say it in daytime language."

Gail Godwin

When it comes to teaching dream interpretation, everyone asks, "Where is the symbols list?" Well, here are basic meanings to dream symbols, but remember that these may change from dream to dream and from dreamer to dreamer. As we have learned, the context of the specific dream will also make a difference. These are generalizations and not meant to be taken as the letter of the law. I have divided the symbols into categories to better explain them. We will go into more detail on all of these symbols in Appendix B at the end of this book.

Trains, planes, and automobiles

When you see dream symbols that pertain to transportation, note that they sometimes carry groups of people. These can represent families, communities, companies, churches, ministries, or organizations, whereas trains can represent movements that are coming because they "roll down the tracks." This could be about a move from God in your life, your family, even your city or nation. A movement from God just means that something new and refreshing will happen. But also notice the context. Are you waiting for a train that never shows up? Was the train derailed, or did it get stopped for some reason? Did the train arrive but it had wings and could fly? These context details will tell you more about the type of movement that is coming.

Planes can represent organizations, but notice what kind of plane and what is happening on the plane. Fighter jets indicate spiritual warfare or military connections. A large plane waiting on a runway to take off is something that is coming but has not started yet. Planes that crash do not necessarily mean there will actually be a plane crash though. Most of the time, it's symbolic and represents the need to pray for an organization or business that is having trouble.

Planes can also represent personal destinies or impact, especially if it's a smaller plane or helicopter. These can indicate that you have influence and can move about quickly and freely.

Our vehicles, such as our cars, can represent various aspects of our life—like our job, life calling, ministry, or whatever we do with the majority of our life. Always take note of the context. Who's in the car with you? Is there anything out of the ordinary, or is there something wrong with the car? Does the car have exceptional or supernatural abilities, or is it a convertible? These are all important to understanding the calling that is on your life or the season that you are in right now. A convertible is an open-heaven time of fun and deeper connection with God.

I remember a woman from Egypt who attended one of my dream training courses, and she never had dreams of being in a car. I asked her what her main means of transportation was in Egypt and she told me it was a camel named Omar. She said that she often dreamed about riding on Omar, so for her, her camel was the same type of symbol as a car is for one of us. They represent our life because they take us from one place to another and we spend a lot of time there. If you dream about riding on a motorcycle or bicycle, it shows that there are aspects of your life and calling that are very flexible and can move in and out and change frequently.

Boats and things that float

Similar to planes and cars, boats and ships represent our own life calling, jobs, organizations, ministries, etc. Ships travel on the water, and water can represent the spirit, so these can be symbolic of spiritual impact. Unless, of course, you have a career or work on a boat, or a boat is your favorite recreation. Then the meaning may change. Most of the time larger ships represent organizations. Again, you want to notice the context of the type of ship. Is this a sailboat? Then it is driven by the Spirit. A battleship can represent spiritual warfare or a cause for justice. Aircraft carriers are groups that help other people with their lives and destinies. Submarines are groups that are more covert and can go deep in the Spirit. A cruise boat represents groups that are fun. You get the idea. Remember the exercise we did of describing a person using a boat? Exercises help us learn what symbols mean when they appear in dreams.

Snakes, alligators, spiders, and sharks

Animals can represent various things. Most of them depend on context and how they function in nature. I highlighted snakes, alligators, spiders, and sharks because these tend to be the ones that appear often in dreams, and they alert us of potential danger.

Snakes can mean that people are lying or being deceptive around you. If the snake bites you, then you are going through a painful time of betrayal. If it is poisonous, then it will be a more difficult time. Sometimes, it can represent demonic attack against us, and these dreams indicate we need to pray and be aware—particularly if it is a King Cobra. This could mean that a high level of deception might be trying to come against you. Remember not to worry when you see negative things because it indicates that you have a higher calling on your life.

Alligators and sharks can represent people who have malicious talk or bad intentions. Notice that both of them live and operate in water, which indicates that it's possible that these people are spiritually oriented but dangerous. They leave a trail of bodies behind them in the form of broken relationships, backbiting, and gossip. I believe the best way to fight against an alligator or shark is to use the dolphin mentality.

Dolphins represent a positive spiritual impact because they tend to be friendly and travel together in pods. Dolphins are the only marine mammals that can actually kill a shark, and they do that in a group together. This is symbolic of our need for community and that love and encouragement always wins out.

Spiders can represent demonic attack and an occult spirit. Notice they weave webs and try to trap things. The presence of spiders in dreams is a call for us to pray and ask God to reveal what is coming against us. They are not necessarily people but could be demons.

Lions, tigers, and bears (Oh my!)

Although I will go into more detail in the symbols list, lions, tigers, and bears are ones to watch for. It is not always negative, but as you might guess by now, it all depends on the context in the dream.

Lions, for instance, are tricky to discern. A lion can represent something negative that is lying in wait to attack you, or it can represent the Lion of Judah, which is symbolic of Jesus and the Spirit of God. Both of them might be scary in a sense. One could be scary in an evil way, and the Lion of Judah could be scary with the seriousness of God. This is not meant to bring judgment against you.

Tigers and various types of wild cats could represent some type of attack against you, but this is not always the case. Tigers and panthers also speak of strength and the ability to survive. Domestic cats are interesting because they tend to be very independent. A cat in a dream could represent someone who thinks independently; unless, of course, you are a person who likes cats. Because our pets are often treated as family members, it is possible the dream is simply about our pet.

Bears usually represent demonic attack against us. Even if they are not mauling or chasing us, just their very presence in the dream indicates that there is a time to be aware of potential attack. There are dark forces that want to take things from you, like your destiny. We also take into consideration cultural personal dream language. For example, a brown bear could represent the state of California, assuming that it is not attacking you.

Buildings

There are multiple meanings for buildings or houses, but they tend to represent various aspects of our lives. Notice who is in them. Are you alone? Are there people from work or your family? This will help bring clarity as to what aspect of your life the dream is about. The most common dream people have about houses is being in their childhood home yet being their current age. This is an indicator that you are either dealing with things from your childhood that are affecting you now or that there could be things that your family is called to do that you will be fulfilling. Again, this is just a generalization.

Even more than just a house, the important part can be the various rooms of the house. An example would be the living room, which represents family, community, or fellowship. Hallways can be transition, while bedrooms can represent intimacy. Bathrooms are cleansing and flushing times. Doors can represent opportunities, and windows can be vision or insight. Basements can be showing you things that are hidden. Offices in high-rise buildings can talk about our higher life callings and destinies.

People

In order to determine what the people in your dreams mean, you must ask yourself several questions. If you know them, it is possible the dream is about them, but don't rule out the fact that they could be symbolic of something else. Maybe it's the meaning of their name, the position they hold, or their relationship with you?

If you do not know them, then you need to ask yourself similar questions. Did they have a name? Did you know their position or authority?

Were they acting in any certain way possibly with superpowers, good or evil? Were they bigger or smaller than they are in real life?

You may need to look up the meaning of the person's name. You can do this in a name-meaning book or do an Internet search. Compare a few to be sure it seems accurate. If it's their position, like your boss, maybe they have authority—that could represent God. Or if they have governmental authority, such as the president, it can represent that new authority is coming to you. Faceless people can possibly be the Holy Spirit or an angel.

If the person is someone you know, but they actually look like someone else, then it is possible that those two share a similar calling, gifting, or have some divine connection together.

If a person's gender is different than what they are in real life, take a look at the change. For instance, if you see a woman that you know, but in the dream she is a man, then this could mean that she is going through a time that will require being strong or tough. This goes for a man appearing to be a woman. This does not necessarily mean that they are suffering from gender issues. It could be symbolic in that the man you are seeing in the dream is going through a time in which he needs to be more sensitive.

If the person is smaller than they normally are in real life, this may indicate that they're going into a time of humility. If they are larger, then they are going into a time of being strengthened.

How to identify what people mean

Do you know them?
Does their name stand out?
What position do they hold?
Have you seen them before?
What role were they playing in the dream?
Are they acting different than they normally do?
Do they possess any supernatural powers?

Clothing and body parts

Articles of clothing can have symbolic meaning as to the types of callings and gifts or an aspect of their personality. It's not so much the individual item of clothing as it is if that item of clothing is missing. Pants can be our daily life or our walk—things we do on a regular basis. So, if you see someone without their pants in a dream, they could be lacking something they need to fulfill their destiny. The same goes for a shirt. A coat can be a major calling on our lives; some people refer to this as a mantle. Shoes can be our spiritual walk and can also be peace.

Accessories—such as earrings, necklaces, or lockets—can indicate gifts from God. A belt can represent someone who has the gift of truth or justice. A purse or wallet can be our identity, especially if it is missing or stolen. Glasses can represent vision.

Various body parts are significant as well. The head can represent thinking. The neck can be direction or stubbornness depending on whether it is stiff or not. Breasts can be someone who is a nurturer. Hands reaching out can be relationship or hard work, while arms can be strength. Legs are similar to pants and speak of our walk. And feet are similar to shoes, indicating peace or the lack of.

Eyes and ears can represent the prophetic gifting. Ears can represent a good listener and noses can represent discernment. The mouth can represent someone who is articulate or very vocal. Teeth can be wisdom and hair can be wisdom and strength.

Weather, tornadoes, hurricanes, and tsunamis

Turbulent weather dreams, like tornadoes or hurricanes, can indicate that you are going through a difficult or tumultuous time. Remember, water represents the spirit, so rain can actually be good. Floods and tsunamis can represent coming movements from God that will impact many people. It will also wipe out the old and bring the new. The interesting thing about disaster type dreams is that we now see these natural happenings on a regular basis around the world, so sometimes it could be prophetic of something about to happen. However, it normally is symbolic. To be sure, it's always a good idea to pray and ask God to protect you and others when you have these types of dreams.

Water: rivers, oceans, and ice

As I've mentioned before, water can represent aspects of spiritual life. Oceans often represent humanity. The beach can mean people, because multitudes are compared to the grains of sand on a beach. But the beach can also be a time of recreation, especially if you live near it. Rivers can be moves of God, and it is important to recognize the context of the water. Is it moving fast or is it stagnant? Ice and snow can represent things of the Spirit that are being saved up for later. Of course, remember that this is a generalization and it could represent weather patterns that may be happening in your area. Keep in mind that sometimes things in the natural realm reflect the supernatural, so if there is a flood, it could also represent an increased measure of the spiritual realm.

Colors and numbers

When interpreting dreams, I put less emphasis on the meaning of colors and numbers than I used to when I first started out. One of the reasons is because there are so many conflicting dream symbol meanings for colors and numbers. I believe that God gives us revelation into the meaning of symbols, but we have to be careful that we are not applying them globally to every dream.

Although colors and numbers in dreams are important, they are more useful in the application rather than the interpretation. Colors bring understanding to context. Remember, if you can take out any symbol of the dream and the dream does not change, then it's best not to focus on it. I have listed some very basic meanings of colors and numbers at the end of the book as a starting point.

I believe that one of the more fulfilling parts of being a dream interpreter is helping people who are plagued with nightmares and bad dreams. In the next chapter we will go head-on into dealing with and even finding ways to redeem scary dreams!

CHAPTER 11

Nightmares, No Reason to be Scared

"Flip it and flip it good!" Doug Addison

Picture this: It's night, you are asleep, everything's dark, and then suddenly, you become aware of something very evil in your dream. It is so evil that you are paralyzed and cannot move! Then, unexpectedly, it is as if you are taken out of your body and you can now see yourself through the eyes of this evil being. You are unable to run or speak. Then you wake up covered in sweat!

People are having nightmares like this all the time, and often they are recurring. I talked earlier about a recurring nightmare that I had from age twelve to nineteen. I would wake myself up and even find myself running in my own house yelling at the top of my lungs. Living with me was interesting! My mother thought that I might have a mental problem and took me to doctors for medication. But it was not a mental problem at all. I realized later, after I had my breakthrough, that it was actually a calling from God on my life and a destiny that Satan did not want me to see. It is very important to understand this principle. When something negative is coming against you, it really does mean that you have something positive to fulfill in life. This goes for your children's nightmares too.

Developing a positive Kingdom perspective

Unfortunately, many of us have been taught or conditioned to focus on things that are wrong, negative, or that don't work. But when we see the world from a negative viewpoint, we can start believing this is reality. If we are not careful, we see the world though the lenses of fear and negativity. The true reality is that God is still in charge and loves us all. God's love and changing power is greater than any evil in this world.

We must develop the ability to see the world as God sees it. You may have heard the Bible verse that nothing is too difficult for God. Reality is that God's love and power are so much stronger than any demonic power. We have nothing to fear. It helps to get the perspective that powers of darkness in this world are trying to destroy God's creation. When we see negative things like depression, suicidal thoughts, sickness and even nightmares, we must realize that this is not the will of God for any person or even ourselves.

It is the plan of darkness to steal life and destiny. Because God's love and will for us is the only true reality, we can recognize the works of darkness as a counterfeit and opposite to God's intentions for us. Most people may not grasp the depth of what I am saying here at first. This truly was revolutionary when I first got ahold of it. And now here's the fun part. When you see the works of darkness in a person's life, or your own for that matter, you have the opportunity to positively turn it around to bring about God's love and ultimate plan and destiny for your life.

> *"… The reason the Son of God appeared was to destroy the devil's work."* (1 John 3:8)

I have trained myself to recognize that when I see nightmares or negative things, I quickly understand it is not God's will. So, God's ultimate plan is usually the opposite of what you see in the bad dream. I have seen the greatest changes happen in my life and those around me when I practice a strategy that I call *flipping*. Flipping means taking a negative situation and flipping it into a positive Kingdom perspective. It is the ability to recognize negative things, turn them around, and interject God's positive will and destiny for your life.

There is a repeated theme throughout the Bible: God in you is greater than all of the negativity around you.[26] To prove my point, science has discovered that there is a major difference between light and dark. Light can be measured and has substance and mass, and when it moves, it has force. Darkness, however, is the absence of light. God is light, and He encourages us to live as children of light.[27] As children of light, we bring God's presence with us everywhere we go, even if we are not aware of it. This will positively affect our dreams. When the powers of darkness realize that you are no longer negatively affected by nightmares, you will see them less and less in your life. Of course, it may also require changing negative behaviors in your life as well.

Developing a positive Kingdom perspective and lifestyle is what will truly change your life and increase your ability to understand dreams and effectively deal with nightmares. I am only touching on the positive Kingdom perspective a little in this book, but I go into much more detail in my book, *Personal Development God's Way*. And I talk about how night dreams point to our life dreams in that book as well.

Recap of the concept

To recap, the Kingdom of God is opposite that of darkness. Satan wants to steal, kill, and destroy, while God wants to bring life![28] We must develop the ability to recognize that a negative dream is usually revealing plans of darkness so that when we encounter a negative dream or nightmare, we can take positive action and not believe that the negative dream

---

26   1 John 4:4
27   Ephesians 5:8
28   John 10:10

is reality. We will not buy into the fear and instead use the nightmare as an opportunity to interject God's changing love and power into our lives.

There is balance to flipping the negative because, at the same time, we don't want to miss an opportunity to respond to something that God is trying to point out to us. Let's say you have a dream that you are at school, and you just took a test and failed. Then in the dream you go out to your car and you have a flat tire. The dream would indicate that God has been trying to get you to advance but you've been failing the tests. Flat tires represent the need for more of the Holy Spirit in your life. Yes indeed, this indicates that you have something positive to fulfill and Satan wants to stop you. But you will need to first ask God to reveal to you what it is He's trying to teach you. Then, you can take steps and work hand-in-hand with God so that you can move on to a new level of maturity in your life.

Okay, now that we have established the concept of positively turning around negative things, let's apply this more specifically to dreams. One very important aspect of dream interpretation is to recognize the dream's purpose. Many dreams are given to us to help change our lives, and once you recognize this, you can change your life with almost any type of dream, even a negative one. My philosophy is if you see something negative, then you need to "flip it—and flip it good!"

Nightmares can be complex

I realize that I may sound as though I am oversimplifying the process of understanding nightmares. And in a sense, I am—for the very reason that the subject can often be too complex to be easily taught, especially in a book. After dealing with literally thousands of bad dreams, I noticed a pattern and found a similar thread in each person's dream story. They all seemed to feel there was something greater they were called to do, but many did not know what it was. This was my story as well.

Keep in mind that as I reveal an easy way to work with nightmares, each person's story and life is unique. It is possible that they are literally being tormented by demonic forces while they sleep. These can come from a myriad of sources such as drug abuse, being violated or molested, or any type of trauma or unresolved conflict. These can be open doors for the demonic to torment a person at night. Nightmares can also come from being around the wrong types of people or from watching certain TV shows or movies that have a bad effect on our spiritual life.

Healing and getting set free of these types of things might require the aid of others to pray and counsel you. But it still comes back to the fact: why would the enemy work overtime on a person unless there is a great destiny for them to fulfill?

Of course, not all nightmares spring from having open doors like I just mentioned. You don't have to have trauma or exposure to the demonic to have nightmares. The bad dreams could be symbolic and God wants to use them to get your attention. Let me show you where I found this with a dream in the Bible.

Example from the Bible

When I was studying the dreams that were already interpreted in the Bible, I noticed something significant in the nightmare that King Nebuchadnezzar had in Daniel, Chapter 4. It is worth your time to take a closer look at this because it indicates that not all nightmares are from Satan and that God can indeed use a nightmare to change our lives. Notice that the dream was actually a nightmare, but interestingly, there was an angel in it. God wanted to use this nightmare to warn the king of what was coming.

"I, Nebuchadnezzar, was at home in my palace, contented and prosperous. I had a dream that made me afraid. As I was lying in my bed, the images and visions that passed through my mind **terrified me** .... In the visions I saw while lying in my bed, I looked, and there before me **was a messenger, a holy one**, coming down from heaven. He called in a loud voice: 'Cut down the tree and trim off its branches; strip off its leaves and scatter its fruit. Let the animals flee from under it and the birds from its branches.' " (Daniel 4:4–5, 13–15)

Daniel went on to interpret the dream and told the king that the tree in the dream was actually the king himself and that he was going to lose his mind and his kingdom for seven years.[29] But the most amazing part is in the verse that follows.

"Therefore, O king, be pleased to accept my advice: Renounce your sins by doing what is right, and your wickedness by being kind to the oppressed. It may be that then your prosperity will continue." (Daniel 4:27)

Daniel told the king that if he would change his ways, then the disaster would not even have to happen. The part about the king repenting was not in the dream. Daniel understood God's heart and ways and that mercy triumphs over judgment.[30] Daniel flipped the negative dream around and offered to help the king avoid calamity. This is a very powerful principle, and we can do it as well.

Steps to flip a negative dream:

- Write the dream down or record it in a journal.
- Use the interpretive process described in this book.
- Pray about the meaning and ask God to show you if there's anything you need to change in your life.
- Look at possible opposite meanings to the negative message of the dream.
- Make a list of the positive and keep it someplace so you can see and pray over it often.
- Take positive action on what you hear from God—like get deeper healing, forgive someone, get prayer, face fears, etc.
- Come back to this dream later and make notes on your progress or new revelation you may have received.

---

29   Daniel 4:24–27
30   James 2:13

Common nightmares

Here are a few of the common nightmares that people are having. Most of these are recurring, and they indicate that there is either a change that is needed in your life or a particular calling or destiny that you have.

The most common nightmares are running or being chased by something evil, being unable to move around, being swarmed or attacked by something bad, being shot at, having knives or darts thrown at you, being in the presence of something very evil, being in a house and someone's trying to break in, the brakes going out on your car or losing your control of the steering, and a violent storm or tornado coming. The meaning of these dreams may change based on the context and the details.

Positive outcome to a nightmare

My friend had a terrible dream about his daughter. A report had come that she came up missing at a lake, and they feared that she had drowned. He was part of a search team that locked arms and swept the entire lake. Then, suddenly, he felt something touch his leg, and his daughter's dead body floated to the surface. He woke up crying and sad all day.

He wondered if his daughter was in danger. After talking more with him, we determined that she was drifting far from God and he was worried about her. I interpreted the dream to be that she was going to "die to herself" and a positive change would soon come to her life. This is exactly what happened. Within a year, she had a spiritual reawakening and her life changed dramatically. The nightmare was symbolic.

Nightmare that reveals something negative

I interpreted a dream for a guy who was having a recurring dream that he was killing people. In each dream, he would pull out swords or knives and mutilate people—some he knew and others he did not.

After talking more with the dreamer, I discovered that he was suffering from bitterness from some things that he had experienced in his life. The bad dream indicated that he had anger and unforgiveness that needed to be dealt with in his life so he could move on.

Nightmare revealing the plan of the enemy

A young girl was having a recurring dream that someone would break into her house and kill her and her family. It was horrifying to her, and she wanted it to stop. Dreams like these often require asking fact-finding questions. By her own admission, she did not watch horror movies and was not involved in anything negative. The dreams started when she was a teenager when her parents divorced. In this case, there was a plan of the enemy to stop the callings of God that were on her family. After discussing it further, we were able to pinpoint a few things that her greater life calling might be.

Dream interpretation is an art that involves listening to people and God. This is such a great opportunity to minister to people as they open their lives to you. You will need to learn to ask the right questions. Be sure to not go by how they feel. Sometimes our feelings can be deceiving. Earlier in this chapter, we read about a man who dreamed his daughter drowned. The dream was so real he cried out and wept over her in fear, and yet the dream revealed something quite positive!

In the next chapter, we will get into children's dreams, and more on nightmares as well as why many young people are drawn to zombies and vampires!

CHAPTER 12

Children's Dreams

"All children are artists. The problem is how to remain an artist once he grows up."

Pablo Picasso

Five-year-old David wakes up from a nap in the car, and while his mom is wrestling the safety straps off of him, he points to the sky and says, "Mama, a buzzing bumble bee stung me and I died! Then, a rescue eagle picked me up and took me to the doctor, where I drank and drank and drank. But then guess what, mama? I came back to life!"

Most people would think David has an active imagination or perhaps that he watches too much television, but there is actually a lot of spiritual significance to this dream. What are the hidden clues about David's destiny? What is the heads-up God is giving these parents?

David's dream is about his destiny and shows that he has a prophetic gift (eagle) on his life but he may have opposition from the enemy (bee sting). But the doctor (Holy Spirit) will revive him. The dream also gives his mom a prayer strategy and insight on how to mentor him in his spiritual life. God will bring new life to little David.

Mentoring children in the supernatural

As parents, we are often looking for clues to discover the hidden treasures of talents, giftings, and callings of our children. As you are learning in this book, dreams can help us figure these out! Just by the very fact that your child is dreaming shows a gifting towards the supernatural and a connection with God's ways.

Children do remember their dreams and sometimes even more than adults. Many children dream of flying, but later in life they no longer fly in their dreams. As we discovered, flying represents high levels of creativity and calling. Younger children have the mentality that "all things are possible for those who believe." As we mature in life, we are encouraged to be more logical.

As a child, I used to have dreams and spiritual experiences, but I did not know how to describe them. I remember waking up on the couch when I was five years old screaming because I saw a light coming at me. My mom told me that I should not be watching TV before bed. Sometimes adults laugh and say our kids have a big imagination. Now, I know that these were legitimate dream experiences, and your children may be having them all the time. By interpreting children's dreams, we can begin to mentor the spiritual and supernatural workings in the children around us.

In the traditional American culture, we were not taught to understand or value things like dreams, angels, and the supernatural. It is really helpful if we talk to our children about their dreams and things that they experience to support them in it. Making it seem normal to have dreams and have open discussions is an essential part of mentoring. Young children do not have language to adequately express the dreams that they are having, let alone understand them.

Here are a few steps you can take to help your children understand and value dreams:

- Openly talk about your family's dreams, particularly at the breakfast table or in the morning. That's when most people will remember them.

- Keep a dream journal for your child if they're not able or don't want to do so themselves.
- Write their dreams down and follow the steps for understanding dreams we have discussed in this book.
- Have the child draw the dream or act it out.
- If they had an important dream, have them create a collage or other artwork.
- For dreams that seem to be important to them, hang the dream artwork somewhere prominent as a reminder.

Children's dreams are a little bit different in that they may not have the same type of language or understanding that adults do. Remember that your child's dream language is going to be simpler than that of an adult. They may see things in cartoon form or associate characters they know from games, books, or superhero shows. Often, these superheroes might be symbolic of angels or even God in their dreams. Pay attention if the dream is light or dark and ask them if they knew what it meant. Here's a good example of a four-year-old child's dream that the parent did not understand but was actually quite prophetic.

Sam's dream

I dreamed that Daddy and me were driving in his car. There was a big bump and the car went boom and Daddy was scared, but then Jesus came and said, "Don't be scared Daddy, it's going to be all right."

After asking more questions of Sam's dad, we found out that he had lost his job right around the time his son had this dream. As I've said throughout this book, cars can represent our career, jobs, or aspects of our life. Sam dreamed that his father had a car accident, but it was symbolic of him losing his job. Seeing Jesus in the dream was reassuring that circumstances would work out, and sure enough, they did. Sam has a prophetic dreaming gift, and we were able to help bring clarity to his child-like dream. Sam, although a young child, truly heard from the

Lord. He may have lacked words to describe the dream in greater detail, but this was due to his maturity.

Children's dream language

It is helpful to keep these things in mind when listening to children's dreams or interpreting them:

- Keep things simple.
- Get familiar with characters, cartoons, books, video games, and TV shows they know.
- Superheroes can represent angels, Jesus, or other heavenly creatures.
- Is there color or is it dull/dark?
- Pay close attention to the sound effects they make as they describe it.
- Notice their facial expression and body language.
- Ask what the child thinks it means

Children's nightmares

I have a friend whose 8-year-old son was having a recurring nightmare that demons were trying to get him. He would pray with his son and tell him that he needed to say, "In the name of Jesus" and the demons must leave his dreams. But it did not seem to be helping him, and he kept having the nightmares. One day they were watching the cartoon *Jimmy Neutron*, in which Jimmy's friend, Carl, was having very bad dreams. Jimmy built a machine called "The Dream-Inserter 5000" that would allow Jimmy to go into Carl's dream and help him fight the monsters. The dad immediately said to his son, "This is how Jesus can go into your dream and help you fight the demons." A short time later, his son was able to grasp how to do dream spiritual warfare—after seeing Jimmy Neutron do it.

I have also seen people do other things for children who are suffering from nightmares. If you instruct your children to tell the demons to leave their dreams and they won't go when you say, "in the name of Jesus," then tell them, "I (meaning you, the parent or grandparent) said they must go." I have seen cases in which the next time the child had a nightmare, they were able to say something to the effect of: "My dad (mom, or grandparents) said that you have to leave." Quite often, the demons leave and the nightmares stop. This shows that parents and grandparents can actually stand with our children and grandchildren in their dreams. I have also seen cases where after this happens, children begin to have angelic encounters and prophetic dreams. It goes to show you that when the enemy attacks someone hard, it is because they have a huge destiny call of God in their life.

Major plan of the enemy

Children quite often see angels and demons and are very much aware of the supernatural realm, but most of the time, they don't have the language to describe what they are seeing. I have been dreaming and having supernatural experiences from as far back as four years old (and I'm sure many before that, but I just can't remember). As a child, I did not realize that these experiences were from God. My parents were not trying to be mean or insensitive when they told me to grow up and stop fantasizing or telling big stories. Back then, there was no one to explain them, but today we are all growing more in our understanding of the supernatural.

I believe that nightmares are a plan from darkness to keep people away from their destiny and afraid of the supernatural. Many highly gifted and creative people get nightmares when they are young. Then they grow up being afraid of anything to do with angels or supernatural experiences. Satan will try to instill fear and anxiety into people, and particularly when they are young, which sets the stage for the rest of their lives. God is not a God of fear, but of love and peace. It is important that we recognize this plan from darkness and overcome it.

This reinforces my belief that when something negative is coming against you, it really does mean that you have something positive to fulfill in life. This goes for your children too.

A young generation of dreamers: vampires, zombies, tattoos, and piercings

I realize this might be an unusual topic to place right after children's dreams, but this is actually the topic of dreams for many teens and people in their twenties and thirties. There is a serious attachment with this generation (not limited to any age) with zombies and vampires. And so it is important to understand that dreams may change from generation to generation and culture to culture. Just as young children have a simple dream language that is different from adults, teens and people in their twenties may also have a different understanding of symbols than that of older adults.

Let's take a skull, for example. To the average Christian, a skull represents death or something negative, but to the younger generation, skulls usually represent someone who's been through a lot but has made it through. To them, that person is an overcomer of death. This may be surprising to many Christian adults but I learned this after interpreting dreams for so many people in this culture.

For a number of years, I have been interpreting the symbolism in tattoos using the same understanding of dreams. It might sound strange to some at first, but I've been seeing an amazing response when we help people understand that God may be speaking to them not only in their dreams but also through the design they chose for the tattoo or the type of piercing that they have. Let me just say right up front that I am not for or against tattoos, but what I've noticed is that about a billion people have tattoos. Plus, the symbolism of the tattoos can prophetically reveal the person's character, calling, likes, and dislikes. I am also finding that the meaning of symbols in the dreams of this generation vary a little bit from that of my generation. I have discovered it is best to not judge things that you don't understand. Accept the person and learn to love and listen.

I meet so many people who are drawn to zombies and vampires. At first glance, you would think that they're just into evil things, but the more I interact with people, God has been showing me prophetic insight into this. Bear with me on this and let's pretend it was a dream. A zombie would represent someone who is dead but yet still living. I believe people drawn to zombies don't necessarily realize it, but there's a good chance that they may not understand their destiny, so they feel dead inside. They may feel like there's more to life. They're barely alive but feel dead.

Similarly, this generation believes that vampires cannot die since they are eternal. But most vampires on television and in movies are not really happy people. They actually want to die but can't. Also, they cannot see themselves in the mirror. This is symbolic of people who do not know who they are or what they are called to do. They lack vision for themselves. I'm not saying that people who watch zombie and vampire movies are bad people. I believe that there's an entire generation of people walking around who don't know what they're called to do in life. I've seen many who match these descriptions, and some unfortunately, are hopeless, and some even want to die, but most would not go as far as killing themselves. So they live life feeling dead inside.

Since we are learning symbolism and to flip the negative, let's apply it here. The zombie and vampire craze is a prophetic sign of an entire generation that soon will find themselves. These people are highly creative and very gifted. Many of them are bored with their current churches or situations and are looking for a challenge. They're not looking for something to live for; they are looking for a cause that they would die for. And just like in the movies, symbolically there is a coming "zombie apocalypse" in which "the undead" will suddenly come out of the graves in masses. I believe we are going to see this happen. Suddenly, people who have not had vision for their lives or know what they want will begin to get it. It will happen in the masses.

Tattoos and piercings fall into a similar category that is greatly misunderstood today. Most tattoos and piercings are considered body art.

They are very personal and highly valued by the person. Years ago, tattoos were only for bikers, sailors, and criminals, but today families get tattoos, both young and old. Quite often they commemorate a life situation or change. They may show a person's values, likes, and dislikes.

While I have been interpreting dreams for years, I've also spent many years interpreting hidden messages in tattoos. I have been having amazing success helping people understand how God might be speaking to them through their choice of artwork and the placement on their body.

By understanding God's hidden language in symbolism; you can interpret dreams, tattoos, and piercings and even discover more about a person based on the types of art, music, clothing styles, and even movies they like. It opens the door to have deeper conversations. My motivation is to see people find their God-given gifts, talents, and their ultimate calling on their life. All of these things will point to their destiny or life purpose on a greater level if you are willing to take a risk and love people. If you are interested in finding out more about how to prophetically interpret tattoos, you can visit my website www.dougaddison.com.

I hope you are discovering how dream interpretation can help change the lives of millions of people from all generations and walks of life. I have so much fun being a dream, and now, tattoo interpreter. I hope you can catch a glimpse of it too. All of what I learned and am sharing with you I got from taking detailed notes after each outreach and event. Now, I want to give you some really practical tools on how to remember and record your dreams in ways that will help make this process come alive for you.

CHAPTER 13

Help me Remember!

"All the things one has forgotten scream for help in dreams."

Elias Canetti

Some people cannot remember much of their dreams; they get snippets and a few details here or there, but mostly, it seems blurred. Then, there are the others who dream in volumes, with great detail and vividness. We all dream—science has proven it—but not everyone remembers all their dreams. This is actually quite normal. I want to introduce you to the idea that it really does not matter if you remember all the details of your dream or not. Dreams reside in the spiritual realm and often come from God. If you study your own dreams, you will begin to see that you may actually be getting more from your dream life than you first realized.

Four levels of dream recollection

I have identified four ways we can remember and respond to our dreams. These may vary based on how you dream. But you can develop this more in your life as you mature in your dreaming gift.

Level 1: Clear recall, clear meaning—purpose is to give direction

A great dream to have is the one you remember and know exactly what it means. This is the first level of dream recollection: we remember clearly and know what the dream means. Dreams like these are very easy to understand and pursue. You can change your life by using dreams that you understand clearly as guidance.

In the book of Genesis, Jacob was given insight through dreams for a business plan on how to prosper when his father-in-law, Laban, was cheating him out of wages.[31] God clearly spoke to Jacob in a dream and gave him a specific plan to take the spotted and speckled sheep and goats that were of no value to Laban. God also said that if he did this, God would cause Jacob's flock to grow and prosper. God used what seemed to have no value to quickly multiply and make a lot of money for Jacob.

Level 2: Clear recall, unclear meaning—have to search out purpose

The second type of dream that we can have is the one that you remember but don't understand what it means. These are the kind of dreams we are figuring out in this book.

Jacob's son Joseph also had dreams about prospering in business but the meaning was partially hidden. Joseph's dreams about his family bowing down and serving him are good examples of this.[32] Joseph had several detailed dreams but he did not know what they meant. He shared these dreams with his brothers and his family, and they got jealous of him, causing him a lot of heartache in life. The meanings of Joseph's dreams were later revealed to him as he actually lived them out, as we discussed previously, and he was placed in high command in Egypt.

---

31   Genesis 29–30, and Genesis 31:4–13
32   Genesis 37

Level 3: Unable to recall—purpose is to bring automatic change

The third type of dream is when we know we dreamed something, but cannot remember the details. Many people wake up with this sense of knowing, but they cannot remember anything about it. This is called a concealed dream and it is actually the best dream you can ever have!

This used to frustrate me, as it used to happen quite often. It was almost as if the dream was being hidden or sealed away, and no matter how hard I tried, I was unable to recall the dream.

There is an explanation for this. It can be found in the oldest book of the Bible.

> *For God may speak in one way, or in another, yet man does not perceive it. In a dream, in a vision of the night, when deep sleep falls upon men, while slumbering on their beds, then He opens the ears of men, and seals their instruction. In order to turn man from his deed, and conceal pride from man.* (Job 33:14–17 NKJV)

God will often use a dream to give us instructions and direction for our daily lives. Because the change we often need is beyond our own understanding or may be a radically different course of action, God will wait until we are sleeping to give us divine instruction. Most of the time, the changes we need in our lives are outside of our current thinking.

So God uses a concealed dream as a way to seal away instructions inside us. We wake up knowing that we dreamed but cannot remember anything about it. Then later, we might have strange feelings like we have been there or experienced this before (also known as déjà vu). This most likely is because we had one of these concealed dreams and then we went and lived it out.[33]

In my live seminars, I have noted that nearly one hundred percent of the people who say they have dreams but cannot remember them also

---

33   John Paul Jackson: Understanding Dreams and Visions audio set

experience déjà vu. These too can be really good dreams. We will later live the instructions out without having any obligation or decision-making. I call it revelation without any obligation. How good is that?

Level 4: No recall at all—purpose is to prepare our Spirit for something

The fourth type is the dream that we can't remember even dreaming, like a dream within a dream. That may sound a little bit out there, but let me explain. Have you ever had a dream and in the dream you say, "I have dreamed this before"? Most likely, you have dreamed this before but do not remember. This is similar to the dreams from God that get sealed away from our conscious mind. We may not remember dreaming, but the dream was placed inside of us and we live the dream out later on in life.

Beaver dream

Let me give you an example of the fourth type of dream. I dreamed that I was in a movie theater and a woman brought in a beaver. The beaver began to run around as if it was busy doing things, but it was actually distracting many people. In the dream I said, "This is the second beaver dream I have had tonight."

In reality, I could not remember having more than one beaver dream. When this happens, we have most likely dreamed this before but do not remember. Dreams can be hidden away and then later revealed to us. The purpose of these dreams is to prepare us for things that we are about to face.

The purpose behind the dream that involved a beaver was for me to become aware! As the saying goes, "busy as a beaver," and I was getting ready to experience it! In dreaming about a beaver in a media outlet such as the theatre, God was letting me know that I was about to get busy in the area of media as well! He was trying to convey that it would be inconvenient and distracting for me. And this is exactly what happened within the next few months of my life. I began to do more television and videotaping for a reality show on interpreting dreams and tattoos. Since I understand dreams, I knew that God had prepared me for it! What an amazing God—through the beaver dream, He revealed the details!

The best way to develop greater dream recall is by writing down your dreams in a journal. I may have easily forgotten the Beaver Dream, but by recording it in my dream journal, I was able to associate it later with my real life. Allow me to give you some tips for dream journaling that could very well change your life.

Recording and remembering dreams

Dream journaling is a must for dream interpreters. If you do not write them down right away, you will most likely forget. Some dreams stay with us as vivid memories, and others vanish right when we wake up. Dream journals can go beyond just recording your dreams. You can use them to track how God speaks, and you can cross-reference them and add detailed notes later when the dream actually plays out in your life.

Tips for recording and remembering dreams

Keep a notepad conveniently located near your bed, and when you have a dream, get in the habit of writing it down right when you wake up. You may want to do what I do: when I wake up in the middle of the night with an important dream I do not want to forget, I make some bullet points on the notepad next to my bed. These are notes to jog my memory later.

You can use an audio recorder if it works for you. I am usually too groggy and can't understand the audio the next morning. Also, my wife doesn't always enjoy me talking while she's sleeping. But if you want to use an audio recorder, you can keep it in the bathroom or step out of the room.

Make a habit of journaling daily. Once you start, you will find that an entire new world will open up to you. I made a commitment to journal every day of the year and now I am hearing God in ways that I never knew possible. God was speaking to me and I did not understand it because quite often, God speaks over time. I'll get into how to journal in just a moment.

A good way to start the day is to talk about your dreams with your family or coworkers. Ask one another, "Did you dream last night?" You'll find that if you are asking each other, suddenly you remember a dream that you forgot or did not realize that you had. Another interesting aspect of this is that you'll find out that others around you are possibly having the same dreams. This will also help to teach our children to value dreams and about how God speaks.

Carry something with you to record your dreams or ideas later in the day. Maybe you suddenly remember a dream or something God had shown you, or a creative idea. Unless you record or write it down, most likely you will forget it again. So, get in the habit of either writing it down, or do what I do: send a text message or e-mail to yourself. I also have a voice recorder app on my smart phone, and the minute I remember something, I make a voice memo. Then, don't forget to get that information into your journal.

Get creative in the way you record your dreams. You don't have to just write them down—you can also draw them out or use diagramming on a piece of paper. With children, you can ask them to act the dream out for you and then you can write down what they tell you, because quite often, younger children do not have the language to express the things happening in their dreams.

Find ways to respond to your dreams. I've already mentioned doing something practical, but you can do something artistic as well. If you have a vivid dream that seemed to mean something special, you could write a poem, a story, a song, or a painting. Often, when you do this, you'll understand the dream had deeper meaning.

More ways to record your dreams

Writing or typing out your dream is the first step. Because dreams tend to be more animated and spiritual, when we write them down we may lose the impact. Writing things down tends to be a left-brained activity, but dream interpretation is a creative, right-brained function. So, remember to write your dreams down and record them, and then you may want to consider one of the following ways to find the meaning. In this section, we will discuss various ways to record and journal your dreams. To see examples of these please visit www.UnderstandYourDreamsNow.com.

Dream chart

After you have written down your dream, take a separate piece of paper, begin placing the various elements on that paper, and circle the ones you believe are important. Then, you can use a different colored pen or pencil and write a possible meaning next to each of those circles. Doing this in a chart or diagram format will help you get to your right brain and see the main elements of the dream.[34]

Bullet point

Again, you'll want to write your dream down first and then go through the four steps that I've mentioned about understanding dreams. On the final step, look for the three to four main points. You can do this in a bullet point fashion. I encourage people that as they are listening to someone's dream, to pull out a piece of paper and begin to bullet the main points as you hear them. This is a really useful exercise and will help you to recognize these points.

---

34   This concept is similar to creating a Mind Map http://en.wikipedia.org/wiki/Mind_map

Whiteboard

My favorite way to train people in dream interpretation is to use an electronic pen on my computer where I can draw out diagrams and pictures and circle things on the text that are important. There's something about drawing your dream, whether in circles, bullet points, or small pictures, that really allows you to see things in a new way. You can use a small white dry erase board for this purpose. In fact, I own a lot of them. I take them with me when I travel. I have larger ones fastened to my wall and am continually using them to record dreams and my creative ideas.

Take a picture

If you draw out your dream or use a whiteboard, you may want to consider taking a picture with a digital camera or cell phone. You can then print it out or paste it into your journal. Also, get in the habit of taking pictures when you see things that remind you of the dream or that God speaks to you. This will get you into the habit of not only remembering your dreams but also interacting with them.

Secrets to journaling

Be sure to record your dreams in a way that suits your personality. If you are not technical, then use a paper journal. Find the best time for you to journal. For me it is early in the morning, but maybe you are an afternoon or night person. The important thing is to capture those dreams and make notes.

As you keep a journal, you can also record other areas of your life. I have a section not only for dreams, but also for daily creative writing, ideas, jokes and comedy, health log, and more. The first thing I do is write out my dreams since those are the ones you might easily forget if you get distracted.

I journal an hour or more per day, now that I am in the swing of doing it, and it is not all at one time. I bullet point things that are going on in my life. It is usually not all that creative or dramatic. Then I go back to yesterday's bullet points, and I begin to fill in more detail as to how God spoke to me—lessons I learned, anything that will add to my life. I spend most of my time journaling in yesterday's details because you will learn more from a future standpoint.

Whether you remember your dreams or not, just remember they may be sealed up. Continue to write your dreams down and keep a notebook by the bed. As you begin to value what God has spoken to you through your dreams, He will begin to reveal deeper insights.

I have more ideas, articles, and instructional videos on recording your dreams and journaling. Be sure to check my website www.UnderstandYourDreamsNow.com.

Now it's time to tie it all together. I want to give you some more insider tips and the next steps for you to become a really good dream interpreter.

CHAPTER 14

Next Steps

"It takes a lot of courage to show your dreams to someone else."

Erma Bombeck

I have presented an accelerated dream learning process throughout this book. It is time-tested and has worked with thousands of people everywhere. But there really is no getting around the fact that to get good at dream interpretation, you really do need to practice. It is just like anything else—you will get out of it what you put into it.

It was not until I interpreted over a hundred dreams that the light switch came on and it started feeling more natural. Something will happen when you get more dreams under your belt. You will begin to notice patterns and symbols, and the pieces will seem to fall together. I have had some great dream mentors throughout my life, and I am forever grateful for all that they poured into me. My prayer is that I can now pay it forward by helping you in some way.

Never stop learning

If I can give you any parting advice that will help you, it is for you to never stop learning. Be a student of the gifts that God has given you, and practice all the time. Unfortunately, many people go to school to learn, and when they get out they stop learning. We were created by God to continually improve and grow. I gave my life to dream interpretation, and after all these years, I have not stopped learning and I continue to practice on a daily basis with my own dreams and the dreams of people around me. Of course, daily journaling is a key.

You will be challenged to find the time to journal and work on interpreting dreams. My advice is to not wait until you have a large block of time. It is best to develop a habit of doing small things consistently on a daily basis. It may not seem like much at the time, but doing small things regularly will produce noticeable results over time. Think of developing your dream gift like working out physically, practicing a musical instrument, or developing a hobby or sport. The more you do it, the more natural it will become.

Once you awaken your gift of understanding dreams, your life will never be the same.

Chances are you will become a popular person once people find out that you are learning to interpret dreams, and you will never run out of dreams to practice on if you ask your friends and family.

Hearing God

Something I have mentioned throughout this book but have not really gone into detail about is hearing God. Learning to hear the voice of God is essential in being able to accurately interpret dreams. By now, you have picked up the fact that we need to learn to recognize symbolic messages and allow the Holy Spirit to guide us through a dream interpretation. Learning to hear God's voice is a lifelong process, and yet it is simple enough that even a child can do it. I am convinced that we all can hear God, and that God wants us to!

I use the following example often when trying to explain how God may be speaking to you, but you have possibly missed it. Let's say you just thought of a friend or family member that you have not had contact with for some time, and then suddenly you hear from them. Or you are driving down the highway, and you get a distinct feeling inside that you should slow down. Then, just ahead, you see the police. How about when you're waiting in the checkout line at the supermarket and you get a feeling you should have gone to a different line? Then you look over, and sure enough, that line was moving much faster! These are all examples of how God speaks to us.

There may be times that God speaks more clearly, but most of the time it comes in the form of a small, quiet voice inside us that, unless we train ourselves to listen to it, can be considered a coincidence. I'm sure that all of us have experienced this sometime in life. Just like understanding dreams, hearing God does not need to be mystical. I like to think of the supernatural things of God as being a natural part of our lives. That would make us naturally supernatural. You do not have to be a prophet to hear the voice of God.

Practical steps to hearing God

Be expectant that God really does want to communicate with you. Most of the time, we simply need to clear away some of the busyness in our lives to perceive what He is saying. He longs to convey messages of love, comfort, guidance, and warning through a variety of different methods. Maybe it is through dreams and visions, through the Bible, through a conversation we have with someone, or through nature, music, and a variety of the arts. The possibilities are endless.

Hearing God requires us to develop a lifestyle of listening spiritually. The best way is to find time to quiet yourself to hear His voice. For most people, this is while in the shower, driving, or simply taking a walk. God longs for us to spend time with Him. Sometimes He gives us a puzzling dream just so we will search out its meaning and be drawn deeper into spending time with Him. We can often miss God's still, gentle voice if we do not slow down enough to listen.

It helps to find specific time that you can listen for God to speak. It really helps to have peace in your life if you want to hear the voice of God. When you are hurried or stressed out, you are less likely to consistently hear Him. It's good to set time aside regularly—daily, if possible—to quiet yourself. For me, the best time is first thing in the morning. I know we are all wired differently, but morning seems to be a good time because the phone isn't ringing, there are fewer distractions, and things are the quietest. After a good night's sleep, we are more spiritually alert. Unless you have children—then maybe it is after they have gone to bed.

Many of us have busy lives with lots to do but we don't have to be hurried. You will go through times when you have more or less time with God, depending on your life situation. A key is to think in terms of having a relationship with a living person. God longs for us to commune with Him like a father would with his children.

Take time to journal and write down how God may be speaking to you. I've mentioned it several times and I can't stress the point enough that journaling will change your life beyond what you may believe possible. Quite often God speaks over time and most people miss this process because they don't track it. Since I take time to journal every day, I am continually surprised to see things come to pass that God had spoken to me. In my opinion, hearing God clearly cannot be done without valuing what He is speaking to you and tracking it over time.

How to recognize God's voice

Most people ask me how I know if what I am hearing is from God, myself, or the enemy? It takes practice to develop the ability to discern. God's voice is not condemning and always carries with it a sense of peace. I highly recommend doing a few of these simple exercises to develop your ability in this area. It might also get you started on using a journal.

Let God speak through writing

Get in a place without distraction. Take a piece of paper or use your computer and begin to write what you feel God is speaking to you right now. You can write it in the first person, like a letter from God, or you can say, "I sense God is saying to me … " Save it and revisit it later to see if anything comes to pass or you get more insight.

Prophetic verse from the Bible

Another fun exercise is to ask God to speak to you though the Bible. Pray and ask Him to give you a specific verse or chapter about yourself. Don't be discouraged if you don't hear anything relevant at first. Maybe you will need to pray and listen throughout the day for God to speak to you. This may take a few times so try it every day for a few days or until you receive something that you have peace about. The first time I did this, I heard God say, "Isaiah 61," which starts out with my life calling in the first few verses.

Train yourself to know God's voice

Go back to the last time you knew for sure that you heard God accurately. Maybe He spoke to you or answered a prayer. Now, study how it came to you, how it felt, and any distinct qualities or characteristics about it. Then, make some notes and repeat the process a few times. It will not take long for you to begin to notice God's voice more clearly.

Do it in public

The more you do these simple little exercises, the clearer you will be able to distinguish God's voice. Maybe you are experienced at hearing God like me, but I still do these types of exercises to stay sharp. After you gain more confidence, go to a public place like a coffee shop or store or even at work or school. Ask God to speak to you something encouraging for a person. Get their permission and share it with them. Notice their response and ask them if it made sense. Remember to try to do more listening than talking. Give them an encouraging word and listen to their response.

All of these exercises will develop your prophetic gift to hear the voice of God. Be sure to be positive and encouraging and use them to help strengthen people.[35]

---

35   1 Corinthians 14:3

Help change the world

I believe that we are sitting on a gold mine of encounters that we can have with people who have had dreams but do not know what they mean. It's one thing to learn how to interpret your dreams for yourself, but it's something totally different when you begin to do it to help other people. There is something powerful in giving your gift to someone else. Also, you'll find that interpreting other people's dreams is actually much easier than interpreting your own. This is because we tend to want to apply our dream before we look at the actual interpretation. Most people will share a dream with you that is usually simple and, in many cases, one of the Common Dreams that I've listed in this book.

People everywhere are having dreams, and many of them are from God, who is showing them their future and life destiny. It is very similar to the cupbearer's and the baker's dreams I mentioned previously. They told Joseph, the dream interpreter, "We both had dreams but there is no one to interpret them."[36] It is not like there was a shortage of dream interpreters in Egypt. What they were referring to was the fact that no one had been able to interpret their dreams correctly. This is because only someone who knows the Holy Spirit and can understand God's symbolic language can interpret dreams that are from God.[37]

With this in mind, it's clear that we are sitting on endless divine encounters with people waiting to happen. This is why I left my six-figure job in San Francisco and have given my entire life to helping people hear the voice of God, understand their dreams, and find their destiny. There is nothing more rewarding than to see someone suddenly make a connection with the dreams they are having to the very thing that they were created and called to do on earth. For this reason, I have trained thousands of dream interpreters and helped launch dream teams around the world. You might say that we are on a mission of love to help open people's eyes to the goodness of God's love and power. We are not like any group of Christians you've ever met before. Our life mission is to

---

36   Genesis 40:8
37   1 Corinthians 2:14, Matthew 13:11

help others and one of the ways we do it is through "dream outreach teams." I would like to recruit you into this new movement of God!

Start your own dream team

Just as I have accelerated you into understanding dreams, I want to jumpstart you into helping other people understand their dreams. Here is a quick way to do that. The fastest way to get a taste of what it is like to be on a dream team is to first become familiar with some of the more popular Common Dreams we went over in Chapter 5.

The more popular Common Dreams you will find with people are: being chased by something evil, falling, flying, showing up late, and teeth coming loose. There are many others, but these you will encounter with people over and over. Now, ask a friend or co-worker if they have had any of the Common Dreams, discuss with them the possible meaning of the dream, and note their reaction. Though interpreting dreams and dream team outreaches are much more complex, this exercise will allow you to experience what it is like to be part of a dream team and see how dreams really do open people up.

Begin interpreting other people's dreams on a regular basis. You can ask them to write them down and give you time to get back with them. Find a partner who has read this book or knows the process if you need help. Develop a short interpretation and share it with them.

Start right away by telling people you are learning to interpret dreams and you need some dreams to practice with. You can get some business cards printed up for free on the Internet. Be careful to not give out your personal information, and always use an email address created for this purpose.

Going public

If you really want to develop more, get a few people together and go through this book with them. I recommend going to a mall or coffee shop and practicing with people around you. Tell them you are learning to interpret dreams, and ask if they have one you can interpret. After you get better, you may consider trying to do a dream interpretation event at a local business, fair, or farmer's market. Be sure to start small and work your way into larger events. Big events require commitment, and leading a trained team can be much more work than you might realize.

Outreach events can include setting up a booth with some chairs and a sign. Name your team using a nonreligious name that seems inviting like Dream Encounters, Dreams Are Us, or anything creative. Use a small sign or menu board explaining what you offer. If the event requires you to charge, you can always take donations towards a notable charity or invest donations into a better booth. Remember, your goal is to help open people's eyes to how God may be speaking to them through dreams. It is really fun and people love it!

Next steps

I consider it an honor that you took time to read this book. Please go to my website and give us some feedback or follow me on one of my social networking sites. Let us know how it has helped you, and be sure to share any stories with us. I highly encourage you to take my Dream Crash Course video training class, which is available online at www. dreamcrashcourse.com. It helps to actually hear me explain some of these principles practically and, in the online class, I give you some more tools and exercises that I have found very useful in understanding dreams.

Life is a gift so be a giver of life to others.

Dream big!

Doug Addison

APPENDIX A:
Bibliography

BOOKS

Dream Encounters: Seeing Your Destiny from God's Perspective, by Barbie Breathitt, Holy Fire Publications – 2010

Dream Language: The Prophetic Power of Dreams, Revelations, and the Spirit of Wisdom, by James Goll, Michal Ann Goll, Chuck Pierce, Destiny Image Publishers – 2006

Dreams: a biblical model of interpretation, by Jim Driscoll, Zach Mapes, Orbital Book Group – 2010

Dictionary of Biblical Imagery, by Leland Ryken, James C. Wilhoit, Tremper Longman III, InterVarsity Press – 1998

Listening for heaven's sake: building healthy relationships with God, self, and others, by Anne Clippard, David W. Ping, Gary R. Sweeten, Equipping Ministries International – 1993

VIDEO COURSES AND AUDIOS:

The Dream Crash Course, Doug Addison
InLight Connection 2012 – www.DougAddison.com

Understanding dreams and visions audio, John Paul Jackson
Streams Ministries International – 2006 www.StreamsMinistreis.com

—

APPENDIX B:

Dream Dictionary

For years, I have resisted the urge to publish a dream symbol dictionary because dreams are often complex and you must understand the context in which a symbol appears in the dream. So, without proper training on understanding context and other elements in the dream, a symbols list will not allow you to interpret a dream accurately. However, it does help to have a baseline or reference tool for some common symbols. Please realize that each of these symbols may change from dream to dream—and be based on a person's own dream language with God.

I have been studying dream interpretation for many years, and I cannot remember exactly where I got all of the meanings for these dream symbols. I would like to give individual credit, but the undertaking to do so would be too great. I learned a lot from studying the Bible and from my personal experience of interpreting thousands of dreams. I owe a lot to the Holy Spirit and my mentor, John Paul Jackson, as well as others who taught me how to think metaphorically and to interpret dreams much more accurately by using a spiritual and Biblical understanding of symbols in context. In no way am I claiming ownership of this list of dream symbols.

To keep this list simple, I did not give any references as to the origin or where a symbol may appear in the Bible. My desire for you is that you would learn to think metaphorically and recognize how symbols change from dream to dream and dreamer to dreamer.

DREAM SYMBOLS

Actor,
actress: famous people may represent the roles they play or possibly the meaning of their names; could be a call to pray for them.

Airplane: they carry people and represent organizations, companies, ministries, or churches based on the context.
- Jet or large plane: same as above just on a larger scale
- Small plane: same as above but smaller impact, personal ministry or job
- Fighter or military: spiritual warfare or military calling and connections

Airport: transition, networking, and connections with other groups; travel

Alligators: people with malicious talk

Animals: various gifts, attacks, life situations, personal characteristics that depend upon what type of animal (please refer to specific ones listed here such as ape, monkey, bat, bear, beaver, etc.)

Ankles: flexibility, movement, connection

Ape,
monkey: mocking spirit, primal instincts, crazy, fun

Arm: strength, connection

Attic: the past, neglected, stored

Baby: something new such as a job, gifting, idea

Back: the past, vulnerability, family values

Bank: money, finances, provision

Bankruptcy: depleted, old season comes to an end, new start

Basement: hidden or beneath the surface, foundational issues
                   or values

Bat: demonic attack, involves fear

Bathroom: cleansing, flushing, healing

Bear: demonic attack, unusual strength
                   • Polar bear: attack that appears holy
                   • Golden bear: California, freedom
                   • Grizzly bear: vicious attack

Beaver: staying busy, steadiness

Bed,
bedroom: intimacy, closeness, rest

Bee, hornet,
wasp: demonic attacks, painful times
                   • Bee can represent anointing or gifting of God
                     because they make honey

Bicycle: leisure, recreation, small impact ministry or job

Bird: depends on type of bird
                   • Songbird: music, worship, joy
                   • Blackbird, raven: undercover demonic attack,
                     negative influence
                   • Eagle: insight, prophetic
                   • Owl: wisdom and discernment
                   • Hummingbird: gentleness, delicacy
                   • Dove: Holy Spirit, hope
                   • Peacock: vibrant, pride

Blouse:	gifting, talents, covering

Boat: organizations or personal job or ministry depending on the boat:

- Battleship: spiritual warfare
- Aircraft carrier: large organization that helps others
- Mercy ship: mission-minded organization
- Cruise ship: fun time
- Speedboat: fun and fast
- Sailboat: Spirit-driven organization
- Rowboat: slow-moving with lots of effort
- Submarine: covert, goes deep in the spirit
- Canoe: smaller impact, recreation

Book(s), bookshelves: information, revelation, education, writing

Boots: boldness, able to go places, walk through tough times

Breasts, chest: nurture, compassion, provider, sensitive

Bridge: transition, season change

Bride: group of Christians, the church, wife, love

Buffalo: fierce, provision, fake you out (as in, to "buffalo you")

Building: depends on the type of building and context

- House: aspect of your life, family, job, ministry
- Office building: business, job, life calling
- High-rise: major life calling

Bull: stubbornness, mean, attack

Bus: small group of people, business, church, ministry, city-oriented or local

Butterfly: come through transformation, beauty, delicate

Camel: perseverance, able to get through tough dry times, connection to Middle East

Candle: light and darkness, guide to others, guidance, hope

Car: various aspects of your life, family, personal job, or ministry; remember to watch for context in order to understand details.

Cartoon
character: fun, consider character's name or function

Cat: independence, strong-willed, sly, creative
  • Black cat: possible occult spirit

Cave: isolation, alone time, hidden

Ceiling: topped out, unable to grow higher, limited, rising higher

Cemetery: old things, dying to the past, family and generational callings

Chair: position, rest

Chicken: food, provision, afraid

Cliff: risk, edge, bigger vision

Clock: time, timing, possibly the numbers on the clock are significant

Closet: stored away, hidden, time of personal prayer

Coat: gifting, talents, mantle, calling, action

Coffin: loss, dying to the old, new season ahead

Coins,
change: money, "change," small amounts of favor
- Foreign coins: influence or connection in those countries

Cow: provision, slow-moving

Credit card: finances, borrowed favor, given favor, debt

Crossroad: change, decisions

Cup: calling, refreshing

Dam: things being held back, power

Dart: attack

Death, dying: leaving one season, moving to another, overcoming things

Debt: overextended, trap or impaired, repayment

Deceased
relatives: bringing wisdom and advice, healing of grief, fulfill the family calling

Deer: gentle spirit, thirsty for spiritual things, food

Desert: dry time, wilderness

Desk: calling, our job, writing, business

Diamond: under pressure to succeed, high value, beauty, influence

Dinosaur: old ways of thinking, dry religious spirit

Doctor:	healing ministry, Jesus (healer), medical calling, need healing
Dog:	friends, love, companionship
Dolphin:	fun, able to refresh others
Donkey:	carries the load, not too smart, stubborn
Door:	opportunity, transition
Dragon:	demonic attack, mystical
Dragonfly:	spiritual warfare gift, something holding you back from flying
Duck:	food, "get down (duck)," provision, letting things go (water off the back)
Egg:	new growth, fertility, new idea, or creation
Elbow:	flexibility, pushing through, working hard
Elephant:	old thoughts and memories, breakthrough, big impact
Elevator, lift:	new levels, advancement, decrease, easy season
Eyes:	prophetic gifting, spiritual perception, seer, clarity
Ear:	prophetic gifting, perception, listener
Earthquake:	turbulent times, radical change, warning of a coming disaster
Face:	true self, identity, honor, self-image
Family:	family values, past issues, generational callings to fulfill, negative connections that hold you back

Feet: foundation, daily life or "walk," support

Fence: division, protection

Fingers: direction, connection, gifting based on which one:
- Thumb: change, administrative
- Index: prophetic, give direction
- Middle: evangelistic, sales oriented, offensive
- Ring: compassionate, pastoral
- Pinky: teacher, instructor

Fire: enthusiasm, destruction, God's power and Spirit, passion

Fish: sport, people, gift to help others, outreach-oriented

Flies: demonic attack, small and pesky

Floods: major move of the Spirit, cleansing of old ways, warning of disaster

Flowers: growth, beauty, make beautiful, gift of encouragement

Fog: unclear time

Food: nourishment, spiritual growth, survival, fun, community and relationship

Forehead: steadfast, mindset, thought life, belief systems

Fox: attack that can be undetected, rob your efforts, attractive woman or man

Frog: attack against sexuality, lust, able to adapt

Front: vision, future

Fruit: spiritual food, gifts, characteristics, spiritual qualities

Funeral:	ending one season, death, change coming
Garage:	storage, rest from job or ministry, taking a break, holding back
Garden:	growth, provision, character
Gardener:	Holy Spirit, Jesus, helper, growth
Gas station:	refreshment, refuel, time of being filled and renewed
Gate:	new opportunity, spiritual connections
Gifts:	talents, gifts, promotional times, surprises
Giraffe:	high-minded, thinker, able to rise above, connect with God
Glasses, contact lens:	vision, insight, needs some type of help to see more clearly
Goat:	negative person, not a true friend, untrustworthy, gullible
Gold:	purity, been through refining process, holiness, finances
Grapes:	gifts, the anointing of God, refreshment, spiritual food
Grass:	growth
Gun:	authority, spiritual warfare, protection
Hair:	wisdom, strength, beauty
Hallway:	transition
Hand:	relationship, reaching out

Hat: covering, protection

Head: mind and thinking, renewed, authority

Heart: compassion, love

Heel: vulnerability, play on words for "heal," resist

Helicopter: similar to plane: aspect of life, job, and ministry, but much more mobile

Fashion: elegance, beauty, influence

Hippo: someone with a big mouth, hurts many people

Hips: identity, passion

Honey: the goodness of God, nourishment, spiritual gifts, God's presence

Hospital: healing, healing ministry, or profession

Hot air
balloon: slow-moving time, leisure, rise above things

Hotel, motel: temporary time, transition

House: various aspects of your life, your family, job, ministry
- Living room: relational, fellowship, community, new life
- Kitchen: place of preparation, nourishment, food
- Bathroom: flushing, cleansing, healing
- Dining Room: spiritual growth and food
- Basement: hidden, beneath the surface, foundational issues
- Garage: rest from job or ministry, not using talents, store up

- Attic: the past, neglected, stored
- Den, Family room: community or fellowship, family oriented
- Bedroom: intimacy, rest
- Porch: community, recreation, leisure
- Backyard: past, play time
- Closet: stored away, hidden, time of personal prayer

Ice: a move of the Spirit that will come later, slippery time

Incense: prayer and intercession, healing, the goodness of God

Insects: demonic attack, more of a nuisance, pesky

Jewels: gifting, life calling or purpose, family and generational inheritances, spiritual gifts

Judge: God, mediator, justice

Kangaroo: unstable or bouncy time, ups and downs, comfort (pouch)

Ketchup: "catch up," running behind

Keys: opportunities, strategies, authority

Kiss: tenderness, passion, love, similar gifting as the person you kiss, lust

Knee: prayer, flexibility, humility

Knife: spiritual warfare, authority, attack

Ladder: advancement, promotion, opportunities

Lamb: sacrifice, young Christian

Lamp: guidance, insight, angelic

Lawyer: justice, defender, mediator, advocate

Legs: your "walk" or daily life, advancement, strength

Lettuce: play on words: "Let us," (asking for more), nourishment, spiritual food

Library: learning, wisdom, knowledge

Lighthouse: spiritual guidance, keeps you from danger

Limousine: elegance, influence

Lion: God: "Lion of Judah," can also represent the enemy, power, strength

Lips: tenderness, speech, articulate, talker

Living room: relational, fellowship, community, new life

Lock: opportunity for later, blocked, guarded

Locust: spiritual attack—normally on finances, demonic attack

Mansion: influence, riches, Kingdom of God, Heaven

Map: strategy, plan, guidance

Marketplace: business, interacting with others, financial gain

Marriage: covenant or promise, commitment, family, partnership

Meat: nourishment, spiritual food for more mature

Mechanic: someone who can help repair your life, career

Microscope:	looking closer, beneath the surface, examining
Microwave:	fast food, lacking nourishment, fast lifestyle
Mirror:	self-image, self-esteem, vision
Money:	finances, provision, wealth, favor
Monkey, ape:	mocking spirit, primal instincts, crazy, fun
Monster:	demonic attack, usually with fear
Moon:	guidance during dark times, reflects God's light
Moss:	idleness, not been used
Motorcycle:	similar to car: some aspect of your life, your job, ministry, but more mobile; recreation and pastimes
Mountain:	higher calling or destiny, intimate time with God
Mouth:	speech, articulation, communication, gossip
Moving van:	transition, relocation
Mule:	slow-moving, stubborn, carries burdens, carries necessities for a journey
Nails:	beauty, fashion, spiritual warfare
Naked:	open, transparent, vulnerable, freedom
Neck:	guidance, direction, stubborn, risk—"stick your neck out"
Necklace:	spiritual gifting, generational blessing, fashion, beauty
Night:	unclear time

Nose: discernment, know if you can trust people, wisdom gift, nosy-prying, inquisitive

Oasis: refreshment after a dry time, rest

Ocean, sea: large move of the Spirit, humanity, great influence, many people

Octopus: controlling spirit or person, multitasking

Oil: Holy Spirit, the spiritual realm, healing, anointing

Old man: old behaviors, things you once overcame, the old nature, an old person

Overalls: time of hard work, willing to get dirty

Ox: hard work, power, slow but steady, strength

Oyster: situation that may produce a spiritual blessing (see also pearl)

Panther: power (negative or positive), independence

Pants: your spiritual life or "walk," what you do on a regular basis, play on words: "wear the pants" (control, responsibility)

Parachute: exit strategy, backup plan, going into new territories

Path: life journey, direction, road less traveled

Peacock: creativity, beauty, pride, royalty

Peanuts: settling for less, not worth as much

Pearl: something small that has great value, spiritual gifts formed beneath the surface

Pictures:	visions, memories
Pig:	unclean spirit, messy, financial provision if in this industry, prosperity in certain cultures
Pigeon:	unclean, taken advantage of, message deliverer
Pillow:	intimacy, rest
Pilot:	leader, Holy Spirit, guidance
Plow:	preparing for something new, groundbreaker
Police:	authority (good or bad), protection, career
Porch:	community, recreation, leisure
Porcupine:	a person that won't let you get close to them, wounds others
Pregnant:	something new is coming like a gifting, job, new idea; see Common Dreams section
Rabbit:	multiplication, fast growth, surprise blessing, sexual attack
Raccoon:	demonic attacking the area of theft, false identity
Rain:	blessing, refreshing time in the spirit, unclear time, move of God
Rainbow:	covenant or promise of something new
Raisins:	gifts or things from God that have not been used (dried up), nourishment
Ram:	spiritual attack, pushy person, sacrifice

Rats: the need to clean things up, things left unattended

Refrigerator: spiritual food stored up for later

Reptiles: possibly someone who is cold blooded or mean, demonic attack

Restaurant: place of nourishment, possible business, career

Reverse: not going in the right direction

Rhinoceros: stubbornness, demonic attack

Ring: covenant or promise, marriage, friendship

Road: journey of life

Robe: calling or unique gifting

Rocket: advancement in higher things of the spirit, spiritual warfare, fast movement

Rollercoaster: fast exciting time

Roof: covering, leadership, authority, protection

Roses: beauty, fragrance, love, commitment

Sand: masses of people, beach, recreation, fun time

School: learning, education, spiritual training, or if you go to school could be your life

Scorpion: painful attack from the past

Sea: large move of the Spirit, humanity, great influence, many people

Seed: growth, God's word, faith

Shark: malicious talk, person with bad intent, demonic attack

Shawl: special ability or spiritual gifts, particularly prayer

Shirt: gifts, special characteristics

Shoes: our daily life and "walk," peace

Shopping
center, mall: business, hanging out (friendships), fashion, vanity

Shoulders: burden bearer, strength, helper

Shower: flushing, cleansing, healing

Skateboard: fun time, recreation

Skates: mobile, gets around easily, recreation, fun time, smooth time

Skunk: unpleasant time, something stinks, bad character

Slippers: comfort, intimacy

Smoke: presence of fire (could be positive), early sign of a move of God, sign of danger, unclear time

Snail: slow moving time or person

Snake: lies and deception

Snow: move with the spirit, recreation, revelation

Socks: peace or lack of peace

Spider:	demonic attack
Squirrel:	storing up for later, sneaky or dishonest, "squirrelly"
Stairs:	advancement, increase or decrease
Stomach:	ability or inability to understand or digest
Stove:	preparation of things that nourish you, spiritual food, things are heating up, "cook something up" (as in to invent something to produce a result you want)
Suit:	business, formal, influence
Suitcase:	travel, change
Swimming pool:	move in the spirit, recreation, spiritual life
Swimwear:	time of refreshment, going deeper in the spirit
Sword:	spiritual warfare, defense, warfare or defender gift
Table:	community and relationship, share spiritual food
Taxi:	temporary time, temporary worker
Teeth:	wisdom, understanding, strength
Telephone:	communication, prophetic
Television:	play on words: "tell a vision," communications, worldwide impact, media connections, influence
Theatre:	creativity, big influence
Thief:	demonic attack to take what you have

Thigh:	faith, strength
Tiger:	power and strength (could be positive or negative), stubborn spirit
Tires:	keeps things rolling, filled with the spirit
Toes:	stretch, balance
Toilet:	cleansing, flushing, healing
Tongue:	speech, talking, gossip (tongue wagging), "tip of the tongue," "tongue-lashing," "bite (hold) your tongue," "slip of the tongue," "silver-tongue," "sharp tongue," "roll off the tongue," "forked tongue," "tongue in cheek," "cat got your tongue?"
Train:	move of God, something new
Treasure:	riches, finances, hidden things, favor
Trees:	leaders, people, provision
Truck:	provision, similar to car, play on words: "pick-up"
Tsunami:	large move of the Spirit, big impact, possible disaster
Turkey:	someone who lacks wisdom, failure, "talk turkey" (talk plainly and openly), giving thanks (grateful)
Umbrella:	shields from attacks, protective covering
Underwear:	protection of sexuality, intimacy, your core level gifts that may be hidden
Unicycle:	similar to bicycle only smaller
Uniforms:	authority, service, careers

Upstairs:	higher level, increase
Valley:	difficult time
Wallet, purse:	identity, favor, finances
Watch:	timing, be aware, intercession
Water:	the spirit, spiritual life, Holy Spirit, the spiritual realm, refreshment
Weather:	depends on the type of weather; turmoil, shaking, change, difficult times
Wedding:	covenant, commitment, calling in life, marriage
Whale:	big impact in the spirit
Wind:	an aspect of the spirit of God, move of the Spirit, difficult or positive time, lift you higher, hold you back
Window:	vision
Wings:	able to rise above or get out of bad situations, angelic, high levels of creativity
Wolf:	demonic attack
Wrist:	flexibility, connection

COLORS (positive and negative meanings)

White	holiness, purity; religious control
Silver	redemption; false humility
Blue	revelation; depression
Red	redemption; anger
Yellow	courage; caution, fear
Purple	authority; false authority

Black	neutral, hidden; dark or evil
Green	growth; misfortune
Brown	compassion, pastoral; humanism

NUMBERS

1	single
2	double
3	trinity, God
4	creativity, worldwide impact
5	grace
6	man's efforts
7	completion, perfection
8	new beginnings
9	fruit of the spirit and gifts; judgment
10	rules, law
11	transition
12	leadership, government
13	rebellion
14	establishment
16	high level of grace
18	provision; judgment
21	jackpot
24	leadership, government
50	jubilee, reconciliation, freedom

Books by Doug Addison

Divine Alliances

Personal Development God's Way

Spiritual Identity Theft Exposed

Write a Book Quickly: Unlock Your Creative Spirit

Training Courses by Doug Addison

Accelerating into Your Life's Purpose

Dream Crash Course

Kingdom Financial Strategies

Visit www.DougAddison.com

CPSIA information can be obtained at www.ICGtesting.com
Printed in the USA
BVOW06s0206171115

427433BV00023B/199/P